The Little Black Book of Training Wisdom

How to train to improve at any sport

Dr Dan Cleather, PhD

Foreword by Dan John

Copyright © 2018 Daniel J Cleather

Foreword: Copyright © 2018 Daniel Arthur John

All rights reserved. No part of this book may be reproduced or transmitted in any form whatsoever without written permission from the author, with the exception of the inclusions of brief quotations in articles or reviews.

ISBN: 1724825801
ISBN-13: 978-1724825803

Disclaimer: The advice given in this book is to be used at the reader's discretion. The authors disclaim any and all responsibility for any adverse effects, injuries, consequences, loss and/or damage as a result of the use/misuse of any information or suggestions within this book. The activities and training approaches, physical and otherwise, described herein for informational and educational purposes only, may be too strenuous or dangerous for some people and the reader should consult a physician before engaging in them.

For Kuba and Max

CONTENTS

	Acknowledgments	vii
	Foreword	ix
	Preface	xi
	Introduction	1
1	Training Theory	3
2	What Are We Training?	15
3	Describing Training	27
4	Progression	35
5	Common Training Guidelines	45
6	The Structure of Training	53
7	Building a Base	67
8	Building Up	77
9	Learning Skills	95
10	What to Train	103
11	How to Train	115
12	How to Train For…	123
13	Recovery	133

14	Intensity Revisited	139
15	Psychology and Other People	151
16	How to Compete	163
17	How to Coach	169
	Conclusion	179
	References	183
	About the Author	187

ACKNOWLEDGMENTS

I have met many of my best friends (and my wife) through my love of sport. Jon, Nick and Raf, our friendships are based on much more than our mutual love of training, but it is fair to say that large parts of this book have evolved from time we have spent together ranting (I may have done more of the ranting).

My understanding of training has been shaped by the many conversations that I have had with other coaches over the years. Some of my friends have had the misfortune of having to talk to me about these things for many hours and they consequently deserve my heartfelt thanks – in a rough chronological order Jason Miller, Raph Brandon, Nick Rees, Rob Palmer, Hayley Legg and Tomáš Hrančík. Special mention should go to Neil Rosiak a fantastic teacher, martial artist and friend.

As will be clear as you read this book, Dan John's writing has been a major influence on me. In recent years I have been lucky enough to get to know Dan personally and the generosity with which he gives his time to people is inspiring – he really does embody his personal philosophy of making a difference.

Of course, I would have nothing to say on this topic if I hadn't be fortunate enough to work with a great many talented athletes and coaches. Coaching people is a joy, and I'd like to thank the athletes that I have worked with for collaborating with me on their sporting journeys. Latterly I have spent more time teaching the next generation of coaches. Teaching is coaching combined with marking essays and so most of the time is just as much fun. Thanks to all of my students who have helped me to crystallise the thoughts in this book.

In addition I would like to give special thanks to those who read and offered comments on this book: Jon, Hayley, Dan, Stephen Patterson, Steve Magness, Pete McKnight, Sarah Kilroy and my Mum and Dad.

Bára, miluju tě. To my sons, Kuba and Max, I hope this book shows that any goal you might set is attainable (be it physical or otherwise), but remember that happiness is derived from the journey not the destination.

FOREWORD

Not long ago, I was standing next to the shot put ring at St. Mary's University in Twickenham, London. It was an oddly hot day for England and my little group of throwers were sweating, sunburning and throwing.

We had a new thrower, Dan Cleather. He was learning the event from the ground up. Now, this isn't unusual as we all start at the beginning, but this was DOCTOR Dan Cleather and he was taking time between lectures to learn how to throw.

I just don't see this kind of thing: rarely do we see someone willing to "begin at the beginning'" and be willing to do it in front of the public. The next day, Dan was organizing an Olympic lifting contest and would later play basketball with his students. He would then get involved with a two-person deadlift contest. Recently, he shared a video of himself deadlifting a massive weight…then passing out.

Of course, he had just finished building, by hand, his home gym. Oh…and he also explained to me the Czech language in great detail walking over to my lecture.

This is what makes us love and cherish Dan Cleather. He is a Da Vinci of the New Millennium. The term "Renaissance Man" has become a worn-out cliché until we meet someone like Dan and realize that the world still has people with infinite curiosity blended with an inspiring work ethic.

In "The Little Black Book of Training Wisdom," you will be treated to the best and brightest ideas in the field of fitness and performance. Dan outlines the theories of training, but he goes much farther: he makes them accessible to the reader, coach and athlete.

A quick example: "periodization is really just a fancy way of saying the "planning and organisation of training". Many books and articles have been written about periodization and each one is more baffling than the last. But, all of us understand "planning and organizing". Dan cuts through the intellectual rubbish bin that has dominated our field for the past few decades and gives us clarity and insight.

If you just need a "gem," try on this: "start light and progress slowly". Dan summarizes the length, breadth and depth of "all of this stuff" that we try to use to explain training with five simple words. I, for one, am stealing this. I laugh out loud every time I think of how Dan colors the idea of "program hopping": curiosity cost the cat his gains.

This book is a treasure and a treasury. Yes, it is scientific, but it is also incredibly readable and logical. Dan walks us through the seemingly complex and leaves us a path to follow to success.

It's a rare book.

From a rare man.

Dan John

PREFACE

The purpose of this book is to communicate my understanding of what makes for a successful training programme. I believe that the book is distinct from many other accounts of the training process for one simple reason. For reasons that I will describe in Chapter 16 many coaches and athletes are seduced by the idea of studying sport science. Their passion is training and the fact that they can indulge this both within and outside of the training environment is immensely attractive to them. However, the very human tendency to overcomplicate things draws people to complex models of the training process. In contrast, the overriding key message of this book is that the training process is inherently simple and is encapsulated in the cardinal rule "be consistent". Ironically, one of the most common outcomes of overcomplicated training schemes is that they prejudice an athlete's ability to remain consistent.

Of course, there is more to a successful training programme than just consistency. However, there are only a few key principles that need to be followed in order to train effectively and the process of training itself should be a simple one. In contrast, at times the explanations in this book itself become a little complicated, as I seek to justify the reasons for my position by reference to training theory. However, I hope this doesn't detract from the emphasis on the simplicity of the training process.

I have aimed this book at the widest possible population of readers that I can imagine. I have tried to be as broad as possible in my descriptions of training such that readers interested in any athletic endeavour can use the book as a manual for planning their training. I have also tried not to assume any prerequisite knowledge, such that the book should be useful to both the beginner and experienced trainer alike.

In Chapter 1 of the book I describe the two important theories of adaptation to training that will be referred to throughout the book. The first is a stress based model of adaptation where the structure of the body alters in response to a training stimulus, whereas the second represents the improvement in performance capability that comes with practice. In Chapter 2 I talk about the targets of the training process, and in particular show that in training we seek to improve either capacities or skills. Of course, neither of these categories is mutually exclusive either inherently or with regards to the mechanism of adaptation, and there will often be a lot of overlap. However, these categories are useful for understanding training.

In Chapter 3 I present a brief overview of some of the common language that is used to describe training programmes and that will be employed through the rest of the book. Then in Chapter 4 I present the key principle that underpins medium to long term improvement in training. Chapter 5 then ties the previous 2 chapters together by presenting some traditional training guidelines for various physical qualities.

The most important characteristics of the training process are described in Chapters 6, 7 and 8. In Chapter 6 I describe the structure of the training week. Successful training is based on a solid weekly structure which is then progressed in accordance with the ideas in Chapters 7 and 8. Chapters 7 and 8 present the two fundamental aspects of a training programme: building a base and building up the level of performance, respectively.

Much of Chapters 6, 7 and 8 are focused on building capacities. Therefore in Chapter 9 I take a more explicit look at the learning of skills, an area that is often neglected in traditional accounts of training. Then in Chapters 10 and 11 I try to bring the previous chapters together by discussing how an athlete can decide what they need to train in order to improve their performance capacity (Chapter 10) and then how to structure the training process (Chapter 11). In Chapter 12 I give specific sporting examples of how the content that has been covered in the previous chapters affects the training performed in these disciplines, and in doing so exemplify the key messages that have been covered.

The remaining chapters pick up on some of the more important details of the training process that have either not been covered in the first 12 chapters or that deserve further elaboration. For instance, in Chapter 13 I consider the role of recovery in the training process. In Chapters 14 and 15 I discuss the psychology of training, and in particular take an extended look at intensity. Finally in Chapter 16 I describe the relationship between training and competition and then in Chapter 17 offer some advice specifically addressed to coaches who may read the book.

I fully expect that there will be critics of this book who consider its content to be obvious, basic or maybe even trivial. In emphasizing the simplicity of the training process I appreciate that there will be a tendency for people to recognise the material here as stuff that they already know. If this is the case then it is fantastic. However, I would caution that the route to greater understanding of the training process is in reflection on fundamental principles to deepen one's understanding rather than in searching for other more "advanced" ideas. I think Bruce Lee expressed this concept best when he talked about training within the martial arts:

"Before I studied the art, a punch to me was just like a punch, a kick just like a kick. After I learned the art, a punch was no longer a punch, a kick no longer a kick. Now that I've understood the art, a punch is just like a punch, a kick just like a kick. The height of cultivation is really nothing special. ... It is the halfway cultivation that leads to ornamentation."

Bruce Lee

INTRODUCTION:
THE CARDINAL RULE OF TRAINING

The cardinal rule of training follows naturally from a very simple truth. If you want to be good at something, you need to practise – a lot. How much you need to practise is less clear. One (dubious) statistic that is frequently cited, and that was popularised by Malcolm Gladwell in his book "Outliers"[16], is that to become an expert at something it is necessary to invest 10,000 hours of deliberate practice. To accumulate such a large number of hours of practice would require a great deal of consistency – for instance, if you were to practise for 2 hours per day, every day, it would still take nearly 14 years to reach 10,000 hours. The cardinal rule of training therefore becomes abundantly clear. That is, if you want to be good at something, above all else, you must be consistent.

The cardinal rule of training is neither controversial nor hard to understand. However, the reason that many people fail to progress in their training is because their behaviour is at odds with the cardinal rule. This is easiest to explain with reference to a corollary of the cardinal rule (note, a corollary to a rule is simply another rule that follows logically from the first). If the cardinal rule of training is "above all else, be consistent", then one corollary is that you should not do things that are likely to negatively affect your consistency. Unfortunately, in training people frequently do things that can decrease their consistency, for instance:

INTRODUCTION

- Train too much or too hard, resulting in overtraining or injury, and thus causing a reduction in, or cessation of training;
- Train too much or too hard, such that they are always tired and the quality of practice is impaired (i.e. they are not consistently practising well);
- Frequently change goals or training programmes meaning that the way in which they train changes frequently (i.e. they don't consistently train the same qualities).

Why do people make these mistakes? In training it is very easy to get distracted by things like new ideas, methods or equipment, and to forget the fundamental rules that are most important to progression. In this book we will delve in some detail into theories of training and performance, and in doing so we also risk losing sight of what is most important. Consequently, I will frequently refer back to the cardinal rule and its corollaries.

"Above all else, be consistent."

=>

"Don't do things that might negatively affect your consistency."

1 TRAINING THEORY

1.1. The stress-adaptation theory of training

By far the most dominant model that is employed to describe the training process is the General Adaptation Syndrome or GAS. This is a model that was first described by the Hungarian physiologist Hans Selye in 1936[23,33] in order to describe the response of an organism to stress. The particular organism that Selye studied was the rat, and they were certainly stressed – starved, exposed to extreme temperatures or made to exercise to exhaustion. Selye suggested that when a stress is applied to an organism, there is first an alarm phase where the performance capability of the organism is depressed, but then the organism adapts to the stress by improving their performance capability. This model is illustrated in Figure 1.1.1.

In order to describe the training process using GAS, sports scientists characterise a training session as the application of a training stress or stimulus. The purpose for applying this stress is to stimulate a desirable adaptation, that is, an increase in the performance capability of the athlete. Over time, the strategic planned application of repeated bouts of training stress can vastly improve someone's performance capability (as illustrated in Figure 1.1.2).

1 TRAINING THEORY

Figure 1.1.1. The General Adaptation Syndrome.

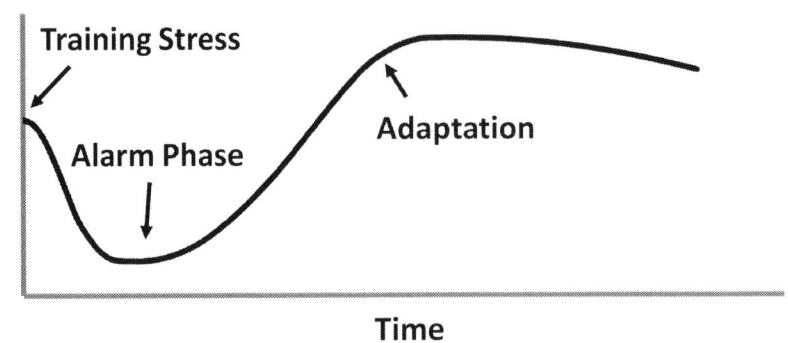

The GAS theory of training implies a couple of important factors with regards to the planning and timing of training if it is to be effective:

- Adaptation occurs after the application of the training stress and so allowing adequate time for recovery to occur prior to the next bout of training is paramount;
- Similarly, the subsequent training session should be timed to occur at the point of maximal adaptation, and not delayed to the point where the adaptation has started to decline.

Figure 1.1.2. Repeated bouts of the stress-adaptation cycle can produce profound improvements in performance capability.

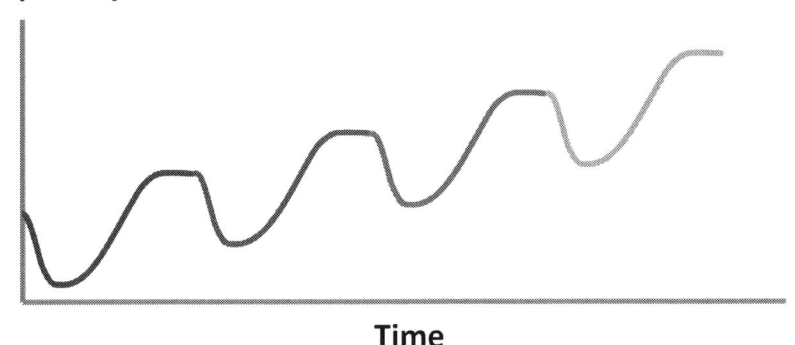

In addition, GAS raises a few interesting questions about the nature of training sessions, to which the answers are not always clear:

- What is the minimum stimulus or stress that results in an adaptation?
- What is the result of a greater applied stress? Is the alarm phase lengthened or the performance decrement greater? Is the resulting adaptation greater? If the alarm phase is lengthened, does the greater adaptation compensate for the longer GAS cycle?

Finally an extension of the GAS theory of training is the idea of super-compensation. This theory goes as follows – if we time our training sessions such that we train before we are fully recovered then we will create a greater decrease in our performance capacity that is called over-reaching. However, if we then permit ourselves adequate time to recover then the resultant increase in performance will be larger – we will "super-compensate" (Figure 1.1.3).

Figure 1.1.3. Over-reaching leading to super-compensation.

Capability

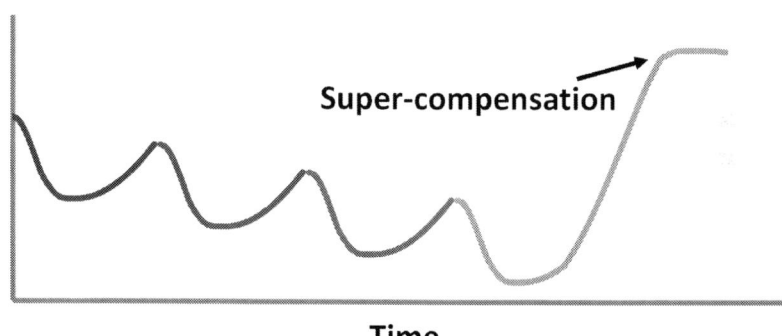

Super-compensation

Time

How do the ideas encapsulated by the GAS relate to the cardinal rule of training then? The most important implication is that if we were to follow the training guidelines that are implied by a strict interpretation of GAS, then the frequency of our training is determined by the amount of time it takes us to recover from training as we should not train until compensation has occurred. If our interpretation of "be consistent" is to train frequently, this in turn implies that we need to do light training sessions that we can recover quickly from (i.e. the stress applied should not be large). If we train more heavily on a given day and apply larger training stresses, this implies that we will need to take a longer rest before training again. As we will see later, in practice people do not follow this strict interpretation of guidelines derived from GAS.

1.2. A note on training stress

It is worth quickly discussing what is meant by training stress. The way that stress is used in everyday conversation implies that a training stress needs to be hard and/or unpleasant. This is not the case when we are talking about a stimulus to training adaptation. Rather in this context we need to appreciate that our bodies try to regulate themselves in order to maintain a consistent internal environment (homeostasis). The effect of exercise is often to disrupt homeostasis. For instance, this could be something as simple as an increase in heart rate above normal. If the disturbance in homeostasis is sufficient, then GAS suggests that the body will appraise this as a stress and act accordingly.

1.3. The fitness/fatigue model of training

Another popular model of training is the fitness/fatigue or two factor model of training[2]. As the name suggests, this model describes the effect of training as being the net result of two separate processes (Figure 1.3). Firstly, when we train we get tired – this reduces our performance capability. Secondly, when we train we improve our ability to perform the task that we were practising – i.e. we improve our fitness in the task. Immediately after training, the performance decrement that we experience due to fatigue is greater than the improvement in our ability. However, as we recover and fatigue diminishes, we find that our performance capability is improved due to the improvement in our fitness.

Figure 1.3. The two factor (fitness/fatigue) model of training.

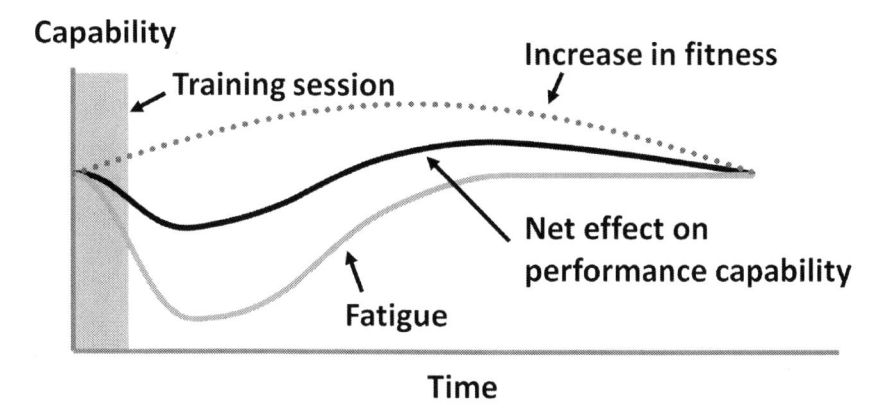

Capability axis shows: Training session, Increase in fitness, Net effect on performance capability, Fatigue, plotted against Time.

What is interesting to note when considering the fitness/fatigue model is that the net effect of the two factors produces a similar overall result as for GAS (Figure 1.1.1). However, this does not mean that the fitness/fatigue model is simply a more detailed version of GAS. Instead, the two suggest different mechanisms of performance improvement:

- GAS requires an adaptation to stress in order for performance to be improved, and the impact of this stress produces a real decrement in performance. For example, a GAS model of resistance training might suggest that the applied stress from the training causes micro-damage to the muscle that produces a real decrement in the ability of the muscle fibres to produce force. However, as the muscle recovers, new muscle fibres are formed meaning that the recovered muscle has a greater number of muscle fibres, and thus an increased capacity for force expression;
- The two factor model suggests that fitness improves from the moment training starts. A potential example of this for resistance training is that each repetition that is practised improves the athlete's ability to coordinate the recruitment of their muscles resulting in more skilful performance. There is no need for a period of adaptation where the structure of the neuromuscular system is changed. Similarly, the only reason that an increase in performance capability is not realised instantly is that the athlete is tired.

1 TRAINING THEORY

The comparison of these two models of training suggests there are different ways in which the body can improve its performance capability in response to training. Some improvements can be immediate whereas others might require time for the actual structure of the body to change. These differences in the type of adaptation will be a central consideration throughout the majority of this book.

The improvement in performance capability due to multiple bouts of training is characterised in a very similar way for the two factor model as for GAS. That is, if an additional bout of training is performed when performance capability is enhanced then there will be a summative effect. Of course, this also means that due to the cardinal rule of training we have some similar implications as we saw for GAS. For instance, this model implies that it is not optimal to train until full recovery has occurred and this carries the same implications as we discussed for GAS. We also have some similar questions: for instance, is there a link between the fitness improvement and the fatigue generated. That is, does a training session that brings a large benefit in fitness, necessarily also create a large amount of fatigue?.

1.4. Practice as a model for training

One of the key messages in this book is that in many cases training can be helpfully described as practice. To some degree therefore, the two factor model of training is useful in characterising the effects of an arduous practice session which results in large amounts of fatigue. However, a major limitation of the model is the assumption that practice necessarily creates fatigue. Such an assumption is clearly false – it is easy to give a range of examples of practice sessions that result in minimal or no fatigue (with the caveat that the session must be sufficiently short). For instance:

- Practising the piano;
- A snooker player practising the "break off";
- A table tennis player practising their serve.

It is true that these examples may intuitively feel different to the common conception of training as they are "practice". However, this type of intuition is unhelpful – these types of session still represent the performance of some type of physical activity (training) that then results in an improvement in performance capability (adaptation). It should not be considered that a necessary condition for something to be called training is that it creates fatigue.

The examples given above have clearly been chosen as they are likely to result in very minimal fatigue. However, it is equally easy to give examples of physical activity that might raise a person's heart rate and get them sweaty (i.e. that feel more like training) but that create very little short or long term fatigue:

- An elite marathon runner going for a very easy run of 20 minutes;
- A basketball player practising shooting 3 pointers;
- A weightlifter performing a short training session with very light loads;
- Most warm ups.

Of course, the question remains as to whether such low fatigue training sessions can improve performance capability. For me the answer to this question is a resounding "yes", and the best training programmes include lots of time dedicated to practice.

It is relatively easy to understand how a basketball player can improve their performance through a low fatigue, shooting practice sessions. It is intuitively harder to understand how a series of easy runs might be beneficial to an elite marathon runner – how might practising running at slower speeds benefit performance? We will see some potential answers to this question in the next section.

"Fatigue is not a necessary outcome for training to be effective."

1 TRAINING THEORY

1.5. Tangible versus intangible adaptation

As we have already seen, the purpose of training is to improve our performance capability. This is achieved by our bodies adapting to the stimuli applied by the training process. The exact nature of the adaptation can be highly variable, and will depend on the training performed and the nature of the performance that we are trying to improve. For instance, if you are a distance runner the performance capability that you are trying to improve through training is the time it takes to cover a given distance. There are a large number of different adaptations that you could seek to attain in order to achieve this goal. For instance, you could:

- Improve the ability of your blood to carry oxygen to the muscles;
- Improve the efficiency of your muscles at producing energy;
- Decrease your body mass;
- Improve your ability to run, such that running requires less energy (improved running economy);
- Improve your top speed.

Some adaptations are relatively easy to explain based on physiological mechanisms. For instance, a desired adaptation that can be promoted by distance running training is to increase the number of red blood cells – this then improves the ability of the blood to carry oxygen as it is the red blood cells that perform this function. Similarly, one mechanism by which strength training produces increases in strength is that it promotes increases in the size of muscle – bigger muscles are able to produce more force. Both of these changes are examples of tangible adaptations – there are clear changes in the structure of the body that explain the change in performance capability.

However, not all adaptations are tangible. For instance, what if a person improves their running economy? This is relatively easy to measure – if a person requires less oxygen than they did previously to run at a given pace, then they have improved their running economy (i.e. they run more efficiently). However, what is the nature of the adaptation that has lead to this improvement in performance capability? There are tangible adaptations that could contribute to this – for instance, they might improve the material properties of their tendons such that they are more elastic, allowing the runner to "bounce" a little more when they are running thereby saving energy. However, there are other intangible adaptations that can also contribute. For example, the person might make subtle improvements to their running technique such that their muscles are required to work less hard. These could be improvements in the coordination of muscles that aren't detectable when watching the person run.

Similarly, there are a plethora of intangible adaptations that take place as a result of strength training. This is easiest to understand by considering the fact that a person can get stronger without increasing their weight or the amount of muscle they have. This is explained by the fact that strength training also results in neurological adaptations, meaning that the person gets better at using the muscle fibres that they have, such that they are able to produce more force using the same amount of muscle. Again, the performance outcomes of such adaptations can be measured, but it is much harder to point to actual changes in the material that makes up the body.

In many cases intangible adaptations will be caused by changes to the central nervous system. These might not then be changes in the physical structure of the body per se, but rather a change in the patterns of electrical signals that the brain uses to control the body.

From a theory point of view, GAS is a helpful model to use to describe tangible adaptations, whereas a practice model of training seems to lend itself to the description of intangible adaptations. Of course, this is a broad generalization and there will be instances where GAS is applicable to the description of intangible adaptations and vice versa. However, in many cases, when we seek a tangible adaptation we apply some training stress, that then results in some identifiable change in the structure of the organism be it local or central. Conversely, intangible adaptations are often most easily understood as us having practised a movement such that our skill is improved, and where it may be much harder to identify structural changes in the body.

In this book I will often refer to GAS or tangible adaptation based sessions, mechanisms or explanations and contrast them with practice/intangible ideas. Again, it is worth stressing that this is a generalisation and that in many (all?) cases there will be aspects of both regimes occurring, however in order to make my arguments clear it is helpful to draw this contrast.

1.6. The dominant training paradigm

Many training programmes are heavily focussed on promoting tangible adaptations. Of course, this is natural – it is much easier to understand things that you can see and touch. This is not the only reason however. In addition, many of the most influential figures in exercise and training have promoted approaches to training that are heavily based on seeking tangible adaptations. As we have seen, the GAS model of adaptation is the most widely used model of training and in particular will be influential on the way that sports scientists and physiologists think about training. As we saw in the previous section, GAS models of training tend to lend themselves to descriptions of tangible adaptations to the training process, making a focus on tangible adaptations understandable.

The influence of sports science on training is apparent across a range of disciplines. For instance, in endurance sports our performance capability is often described in terms of a range of variables that are readily measured and that clearly relate to tangible adaptations. For instance, endurance athletes are very interested in improving their "VO_2 max". This is a measure of the maximum amount of oxygen that can be used by the body during exercise, and is influenced by tangible adaptations like the amount of oxygen that can be carried in the blood, and the capability of the muscles to use oxygen to create energy. It is not hard to see how a focus on these types of physiological measures then leads to a focus on the tangible adaptations that improve them.

In recent years sports scientists have begun to recognise the importance of intangible adaptations. In endurance running an important intangible adaptation is running economy and we know that better runners are more economical[24,32]. Despite this however, in many running programmes it is hard to identify training elements that are explicitly focussed on improving running economy.

Within resistance training one of the most influential figures is Arnold Schwarzenegger. Schwarzenegger contributed to the popularity of bodybuilding and wrote extensively on training. Bodybuilding is a sport that is entirely predicated on tangible adaptations – the aim is to change the size and shape of the muscles. It is no surprise therefore that bodybuilding approaches to training are heavily influenced by GAS – there is a focus on causing as much muscle damage as possible to impose a very large stress, and on targeting the specific structures where change is desired. This approach to training continues to be widely practised even when a trainee's goals are not driven by aesthetic considerations.

Of course, there are training philosophies that are less extremely focussed on tangible adaptations. For instance, a common training maxim within strength and conditioning circles is "to train movement, not muscles". This is clearly a direct reaction to the bodybuilding approach, and reflects the idea that in performance it is the quality of movement, a more intangible concept, that is important, not the size of the engine per se. Despite this however, even training approaches that are focussed on movement often tend to be heavily influenced by GAS considerations.

I am not arguing here that GAS influenced approaches to training that seek tangible adaptations are wrong – quite the opposite. The application of training stresses to create structural changes in the body is a very important part of the training process. Rather my argument here is that many training approaches neglect a consideration of practice and intangible adaptations, or don't pay sufficient attention to these methods of performance enhancement. This is a grave error as intangible adaptations can also be powerful drivers of improvements in performance capability. Much of the discussion in this book revolves around the inter-relation of these two approaches in order to create training approaches that most optimally adhere to the cardinal rule of training.

2 WHAT ARE WE TRAINING?

2.1. Skills and capacities

So far we have talked about training to increase our performance capability. This is a clearly quantifiable aim – we want our competitive results to improve. However, if we only consider our overall performance capability it limits our ability to identify the training that we need to do to improve. Instead, we need to recognise that almost all sporting performances are multi-factorial and that our overall performance capability is actually the product of various more fundamental human abilities. It is the purpose of this chapter to identify these abilities in order that we can then talk about how they are most effectively trained.

In this chapter when I talk about the fundamental human abilities that are commonly targeted by training I will distinguish between "skills" and "capacities." In this context, a skill reflects the athlete's ability to control their body accurately, efficiently and in a timely manner. Conversely, a capacity is the athlete's ability to express a given quality – for instance, the maximum force they can express, the range of motion of their joints, or the amount of time that they can sustain a given task. In many cases improvements in skill will be made through intangible adaptations whereas improvements in capacity will be made through tangible adaptations.

I will make the generalisation that we express our capacities when we perform a particular skill. However it is important to recognise that this is to some degree an arbitrary classification and that there will often be a great deal of crossover between skills and capacities. Sometimes it will be hard to identify where the skill ends and the capacity begins. For instance, the ability to express maximum force is a capacity that is related to the size of a person's muscles and one tangible adaptation from training is an increase in muscle size. However, the ability to express force in a particular movement is also a skill. A person with a skilful technique will be able to more effectively coordinate their body to express higher levels of force. Similarly, there are a number of neural adaptations to strength training that are probably best described as intangible adaptations that also result in an increase in the ability to express maximum force.

2.2. Ability to express force (capacity/skill)

"By understanding force, we can achieve enlightenment."

Wang Zongyue, The Canon of Tai Chi Chuan,
Translated by Dan Docherty

If asked to give a definition of "strength" a common definition would be "the ability to express force". However, I have mindfully not named the quality described in this section as strength because for most people strength connotes the ability to express high levels of force. Such a restricted definition does not do justice to the variety of different factors involved in force expression. Similarly, the ability to express force is much more important than simply describing a person's ability to move a heavy external load.

Of course, in some sports a person's ability to express a high level of force is a key performance variable. However, reaching a maximum level of force production takes time (an oft quoted statistic is that it takes over 0.3s for a muscle to go from relaxed to maximal force production[1]). In many sports the amount of time that is available to express force is strictly limited (for instance in sprinting the foot is only in contact with the ground for approximately 0.1s[37]). Thus the speed with which a person is able to generate force (for instance, the peak force that a person can reach in 0.2s) is arguably as important as the maximum force they are able to exert when time is not limited (the two variables often show some degree of correlation however). This quality is normally referred to as their rate of force development (RFD).

In fact, the picture is actually a little more complicated even than this. The most important variable to consider is the "total" force expressed in a given movement. How can we calculate total force? Figure 2.2 is a graph of the force exerted by a person during a vertical jump with force on the y-axis and time on the x-axis. One measure of the total force expressed is the area under the curve – this is the total force expressed with regards to time and is called impulse. On Figure 2.2 the net impulse is indicated by the area that is shaded and is the total impulse minus the impulse that is simply due to a person's weight. The net impulse is a particularly important variable because it is perfectly related to a person's change in velocity during a movement – more impulse equals a greater change in velocity. Often sporting performance is predicated on making the largest possible changes in velocity in the limited amount of time that is available which is largely a function of the ability to create a large amount of net impulse.

Figure 2.2. Net impulse during vertical (squat) jumping (shaded region).

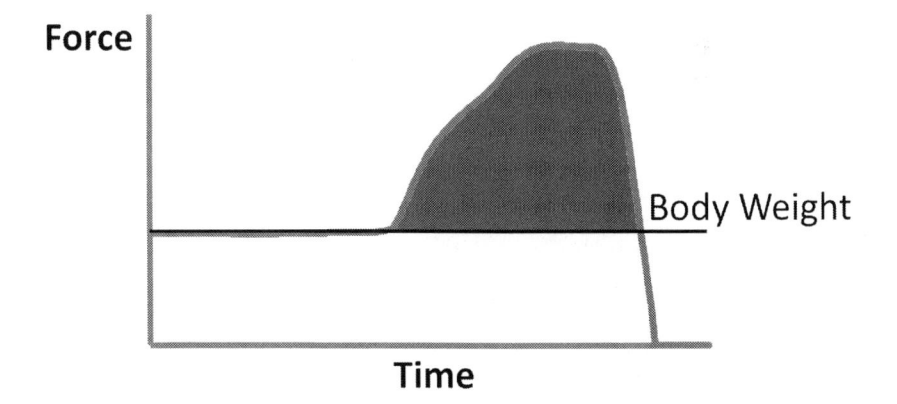

In Figure 2.2, the RFD is represented by the gradient of the curve. It is thus visually obvious why RFD is so important – the steeper the gradient of the curve the larger the area underneath it. The other determinant of the area under the curve is the length of time that force is expressed. In some movements more skilful performers are also able to express force for a longer period of time (provided this is advantageous in the sport itself). For instance, the gross motor pattern that we all use in order to jump vertically is to rely more on the hip joint in the early part of the jump, the knee in the middle, and the ankle towards the end. This pattern is chosen because it allows us to prolong the amount of time we are in contact with the floor while still attempting to exert the highest forces that we can[8].

When we understand the relationship between net impulse and change in velocity we find that many of the capacities that people train to improve are really just variants of the ability to express force or net impulse. For instance:

- A person's acceleration capability, that is their ability to increase their velocity, is almost by definition a function of their ability to create net impulse. Note that in this context acceleration also includes deceleration;
- A person's maximum speed capability is dependent on how quickly they can generate the vertical impulse required to propel themselves back into the air, on each step, during high speed running;
- A person's change of direction capability is a function of their ability to decelerate and then reaccelerate in a new direction, and thus a function of net impulse;
- How high a person can jump is a function of their vertical take-off velocity, and thus directly related to their impulse capability;
- How far a person can throw is a function of the velocity of the hand at the point of release and thus directly related to the impulse they apply to the implement being thrown.

Even capabilities that people don't generally equate with force expression are highly influenced by these considerations. For instance, to run a 4 minute mile requires an athlete to run each 100 metre stretch in under 15 seconds. This is faster than many people's absolute top speed, indicating that elite middle distance running is also highly dependent on a person's ability to express force.

Similarly, within training it is common for people to train to be more "powerful", or to increase their "power output". However, power is also a property that is related to force expression. In this case, power represents the ability to express relatively higher forces when moving at a relatively higher speed.

What we have seen here is that many of the capabilities that people train for (e.g. acceleration, velocity, agility, power) are just variations of a person's ability to express force – for this reason these capabilities are not described as separate skills or capacities in this section. Where these capabilities do differ is in the movement in which they are expressed. This then is the reason why people often train differently when training for different skills like maximum velocity or jump height – they need to practise the skill and get good at expressing force in the particular positions, muscular contraction regimes etc involved in the skill. However it is critically important to remember that the capacity that determines the ultimate performance within the skill is the ability to express force.

2.3. Endurance (capacity)

When we refer to a person's endurance we are generally talking about their ability to sustain their performance in a given task at a particular intensity. Thus endurance relates to the length of time that a person can maintain a particular activity, or how quickly they can complete a particular task where the task is of reasonable duration. In most cases endurance can also be described in terms of the "total" force expressed - the exceptions are where there is no movement or limited movement, or when an activity is performed deliberately slowly. For endurance we are often interested in the total amount of "work" done and/or the amount of work done in a particular time period ("work" is a combination of the amount of force expressed and the distance moved).

There are broadly three factors that affect a person's endurance:

- The capacity of the body to release energy;

- The capacity of the body to continue working effectively after several contractions or as the waste products generated by exercise begin to accumulate;
- Psychological factors – in particular a person's ability to tolerate the pain and discomfort associated with maximal and near maximal endurance performances.

The body accesses energy by breaking down adenosine triphosphate (ATP). There are three energy pathways by which the body can create ATP for energy. Firstly, a small amount of ATP is stored in the muscles and the body has a limited capability to resynthesize this from stores of creatine phosphate in muscle. Secondly and thirdly, the body can create ATP from its glycogen stores either in the absence (anaerobic) or presence (aerobic) of oxygen. Anaerobic metabolism is faster, cannot be sustained for as long and produces lactic acid. Generally during activity all three energy pathways will be involved, but their relative contributions will depend on the nature and duration of the activity. The most explosive activities rely more heavily on stored ATP, whereas the longest duration, lower intensity activities predominantly engage the aerobic system. Because each energy pathway is distinct, different training methods should be employed to most optimally target adaptations in each of them. However, it is worth remembering that because all three pathways will be involved in any activity most endurance training activities will provide a benefit to all of them.

Muscular endurance is a quality that is distinct from the three energy pathways described above, and broadly describes the ability of the muscles to continue producing forceful contractions. Again, there are a number of factors that affect a person's muscular endurance and therefore the mode of training will vary depending on the targeted factor. For instance, there are a number of different types of muscle fibre that have different properties – and thus a viable strategy is to train to increase the proportion of fibres with better muscular endurance properties.

Finally, when talking about endurance it is also worth mentioning "work capacity". In this context this describes the amount of training that a person can do before their fatigue reaches a given level and/or compels them to stop. This is not simply a function of their ability to access energy, but will also include muscular and psychological factors.

2.4. Mobility (capacity)

Mobility can be defined as the range of motion of a joint that is available to a person during movement. It is determined by multiple factors, some of which are very trainable. Of course, the genetic heritage of a person does set some upper limits on their potential mobility. For instance, the structure of a joint is a clear constraint – you can't move one bone through an adjacent bone. The trainable factors include both structural and neural factors. From a structural point of view, the material properties of muscles and connective tissues can be altered through training such that they provide less passive resistance to movement – these are clear tangible adaptations. However, the neural system also controls the potential range of motion of the joints during movement to minimise injury risk. Thus training for improved mobility should also address these factors to ensure that any improvements in the potential mobility of the joints can be accessed during movement.

2.5. Loading capacity

During movement the bones, muscles, and connective tissues of the body experience a loading as a result of the forces expressed. The loading capacity of the body describes the tolerance of these structures to this loading. In particular, we know that forces can injure these structures either if a one-off force is too high (acute injury) or through repetitive loading (chronic injury).

There are a number of factors that affect loading capacity. Clearly if a person is already suffering from some sort of injury then their loading capacity will be reduced. Similarly, a person's loading history is important in understanding their capacity to tolerate future loading.

The structural properties of the bones, muscles and connective tissues are important in understanding loading capacity. For instance, for a given loading scenario, the more muscle tissue you have, the more this loading can be shared among muscle fibres reducing the force they experience. Similarly, the density of a bone is a key factor in determining how much force is required to break it. These structural properties will change in response to an adaptive stress (a clear tangible adaptation), making loading capacity eminently trainable.

The nervous system is also important in understanding loading capacity. For instance, there are a number of regulatory mechanisms that the body uses to control the amount of loading experienced by muscles and tendons. These mechanisms can also be affected by training. In many cases this will amount to a predominantly intangible adaptation.

Training that is primarily designed to increase loading capacity is often called conditioning. Again, the training that is performed will be highly dependent upon the desired effect and/or the structure or system being targeted.

2.6. Movement skill

It is harder to define movement skill than one might first imagine, especially if one is aware of avoiding tautologies such as "movement skill is the ability of an athlete to move skilfully". One of the difficulties arises because the performance goals of movement tasks can be so different. For instance, for a dancer a high level of movement skill indicates an ability to perform a large variety of complex movement patterns in an aesthetically pleasing manner. In contrast, for a shot putter high levels of movement skill would mean that they are able to use their force expression capabilities to project a shot for maximum distance. In this case, aesthetics are largely irrelevant except for a select community of throwers who appreciate the technical beauty of such a skill. For an archer or darts player, high levels of skill are also manifested in the effect of the performer on the environment rather than being inherent to the movement itself as is the case for the dancer, but in this case the accuracy of the outcome is of key importance.

There is a large body of research literature that has sought to understand skill development. It is generally accepted that less skilful movements are performed under the conscious cognitive control of the athlete, whereas the movements of more skilful performers are unconscious and automatic. In addition, the highest level of skill is a movement that is both automatic and that doesn't break down under external pressure.

It used to be common to consider that the hallmark of expert performance of a skill was the production of a pattern of movement that was unaltered from one repetition to the next. It is now considered that expert performers actually exhibit variability in the execution of skills, but that there are fundamental aspects of the movement that remain stable within each repetition. Variability in movement is thought to be important to allow expert performers to modify their skill based on the demands of the performance environment. The consequences of these ideas for the training of skills will be discussed in Chapter 9.

2.7. Movement economy (skill)

Movement economy is the efficiency of an athlete in performing a skill. In many cases efficiency is taken to mean the energy cost of performing a given movement - less energy usage being synonymous with better economy. In some sports, movement economy can be a deciding factor in competitive performance. For instance, in distance running the aerobic capacities of elite athletes are often very similar and instead it is running economy that can account for differences in performance at this level[12,24]. There is evidence that strength training can improve running economy[6], and this is probably mediated both by tangible and intangible factors. Running economy is therefore a good example of the blurred lines between skills and capacities.

In this book I have chosen to present an athlete's movement economy as a separate entity to their movement skill. This is to some degree an arbitrary distinction, but my rationale for this is as follows. It is entirely possible to have a high level of movement skill without the movement being particularly economical. The degree to which this is important will depend on the nature of the sporting goal. For instance, consider flat water canoeing which at Olympic level is contested at both sprint (200m) and middle distances (1000m). Clearly, athletes in both disciplines have a high level of specific canoeing movement skill. However, the economy of movement is much more important in the longer event (the 200m race lasts around 40s in comparison to the 3½ to 4 minute 1000m race). Of course, in sports like distance running an athlete's economy might be the key aspect of their movement skill. However, even in this case the subtle differences in technique that indicate a more economical skill may not be obviously visually apparent and assessment of economy often requires individual physiological testing.

2.8. Decision making (skill)

Skills are not just manifested in the ability to control the body, but also in the mental processes that govern movement (in fact, the control of the body is really just another mental process too, but that is a different argument). For instance, reaction time is a quality that will often appear in a traditional list of athletic skills. The ability to quickly process information from the competitive environment and then make the best decisions is a very influential aspect of performance particularly in open movements where the athlete has to respond to external stimuli.

A good example of the importance of decision making is exemplified by considering the performance capability that is often described as agility. Contemporary accounts of agility now recognise agility performance as being dependent upon two different capacities or skills. The first is the ability of the athlete to perform a pre-planned set of movements in the fastest time possible. This ability is tightly linked to the ability to express force. However, the transfer of this ability into the competitive environment is dependent upon the athlete's decision making skill.

2.9. Expectation: nature versus nurture

The degree to which a person's abilities or behaviours are genetically predetermined or can be cultivated through their upbringing and environment is a contentious debate across a wide variety of disciplines. This question is of key relevance when trying to assess a person's potential in a given physical activity. Certainly there are genetic factors that are highly influential in determining our baseline skills and capacities. For instance, the proximity of a muscle's attachment to the centre of the joint of the bone that it moves influences the amount of force that a person can exert on the external environment and cannot be changed through training. Similarly, if you spend your adolescence at high altitude, you will grow up with permanent physiological adaptations that improve your endurance performance.

Despite the influence of these largely unchangeable factors, our performance capabilities are much more malleable than people tend to think. In many cases we are able to substantially change our capacities (just think of the prodigious gains in muscle size attained by bodybuilders). In addition, the expression of these capacities is a skill that can be learned and perfected to a very great degree (think of the level of skill attained by an elite tennis player and remember that no one is born knowing how to play tennis). One's expectation when starting training should be that it is possible to very substantially improve their performance capability.

Finally, it is worth pointing out that the relative contributions of nature and nurture to our abilities is far from being known. Given this uncertainty, it is much more positive to have an attitude which gives primacy to nurture, as this can inspire us to believe in our capacity to rise to any challenge. On the contrary, believing in the dominance of nature is an inherently self-limiting perspective.

3 DESCRIBING TRAINING

3.1. Introduction

In this chapter I will introduce some of the common language that people use to describe training programmes. Consequently, this chapter is mainly just definitions, but these are necessary in order to understand the chapters that follow.

3.2. Training mode and task

If we are to describe a training programme, the first thing we need to be able to describe is the "type" of training that we are doing. In this book I will use a two tier system in order to specify this. First of all we need to specify the training mode – these are categories like resistance training, endurance training or flexibility training. Secondly, within each training mode there are a variety of different training tasks. For instance, within the resistance training mode there are a plethora of different exercises that can be performed.

3.3. Volume

Volume and intensity are by far the most common "variables" that are used to describe training programmes. This should make intuitive sense – volume is a measure of how "much" was done, whereas intensity is a measure of how "hard" it was. These two factors clearly have a lot of potential for describing how stressful a particular activity is for the body.

It is not a trivial task to quantify how much training has been done. Probably the most general way of quantifying how much training was performed is simply to count the total duration of training over a given period in terms of minutes and hours. However in practice measures of volume often tend to be specific to the training mode or task. For example:

- For activities which are endurance based, one of the most common methods of quantifying volume is by measuring the distance that was covered over a given period. For instance, distance runners, cyclists, rowers, swimmers and canoeists will all track weekly mileage;
- For activities which involve the performance of some type of repetitive movement (e.g. resistance training) it is common to count the number of repetitions.

Of course, a measure of volume can just give a "headline" figure as to the quantity of work that was performed over a given period. However, more detailed accounts of the volume of training can give a reasonably clear picture as to the structure of training, and even the goals of a particular training programme. For instance, in resistance training, the total number of repetitions performed is dependent on the number of "sets" that were performed for each exercise and the number of repetitions performed in each set. Figure 3.3 illustrates the training volume for two different resistance training sessions in terms of the sets and repetitions of each exercise, where the exercises themselves are identical between the sessions. However, the sets and repetitions for each session tell us that the first one is aimed at building muscle size whereas the second targets strength.

Figure 3.3. Sets and repetitions for example hypertrophy (muscle building) and strength training sessions.

Exercise	Hypertrophy	Strength
Back Squat	4 × 12	6 × 3
Romanian Deadlift	3 × 10	4 × 6
Bench Press	4 × 12	6 × 2
Bent Over Row	4 × 12	5 × 5
Core		

3.4. Intensity

As seen in the previous section, intensity is the variable that is used to describe how hard a person is working in a given task or training session. This is generally done by comparison to the maximum performance capability of the athlete. For example, in resistance training intensity is often defined by reference to a person's 1 repetition maximum (1RM). That is, if we know the maximum weight that a person can lift in a given exercise, then we can express the intensity of activity relative to this weight. Intensity is then expressed as a percentage of 1RM. For instance, if my 1RM in the bench press is 100kg and I perform a set with 80kg, then I am working with an intensity of 80% of 1RM.

The measure that is chosen to represent intensity needs to be consistent with the goal of training. For example, in endurance training it is common for the intensity of training to be expressed relative to a person's maximum heart rate. Clearly, the closer the heart rate is to maximum, the harder a person is working. This definition of intensity might be useful for quantifying endurance training, as it provides some type of estimation of the stresses that are exerted on the aerobic and anaerobic energy systems. However, it will not be appropriate for describing the intensity of training that is focused on maximal speed development. For instance, the speed at which I can complete a maximal 100m sprint will be greater than during a

3 DESCRIBING TRAINING

1000m run. However, my heart rate will almost certainly be higher in the latter session. If my goal is to improve my maximum speed then it seems more relevant to quantify the intensity of exercise relative to my maximum speed, than my maximum heart rate.

It is also important to note that although intensity is often expressed as a percentage of some type of maximum, that this does not necessarily mean that the scale is linear. For instance, in endurance training it is common to define different "zones of training" (see an example in Chapter 5.3). However, these zones are nominally meant to represent changes in the way in which energy is being produced. This is often quantified by reference to the blood lactate level of the athlete. However, blood lactate is hard for an individual to measure in every training session. Consequently, physiological testing can be used to find the relationship between blood lactate level and heart rate (Figure 3.4). However it should be noted that there is not a linear relationship between heart rate and blood lactate.

Figure 3.4. Relationship between blood lactate level and heart rate as exercise intensity is increased.

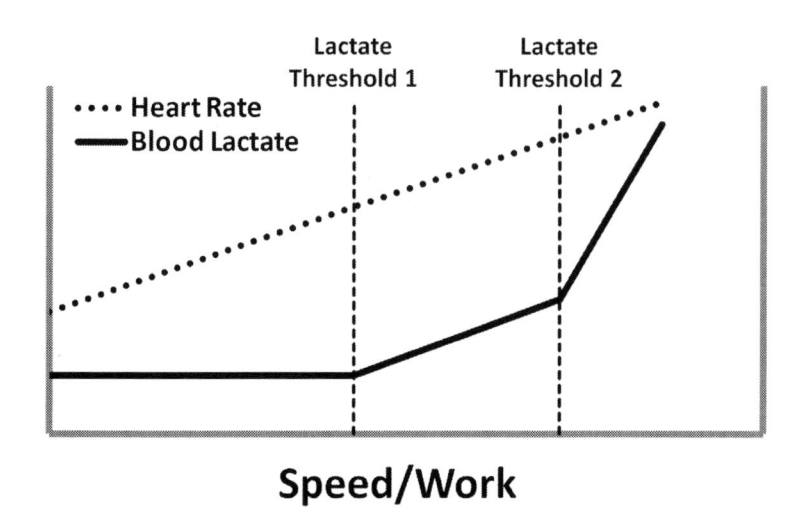

The intensity of activity can also be described based upon the athlete's own perception of how hard they are working. A common tool that is used to perform this assessment is the Borg Rating of Perceived Exertion (RPE)[9].

Of course, there are some self evident problems with such subjective ratings of exercise intensity, but they still represent an excellent way to describe intensity.

So far I have described intensity as the performance of an athlete relative to some measure of their maximum capability. In the English vernacular, intensity can also have other meanings that relate to a person's focus or emotional investment in a task. These alternative descriptions of intensity are also of pivotal importance to the understanding of training, but will not be discussed here. Instead I will return to questions of intensity in Chapter 14.

3.5. Rest/recovery

There are various different rest/recovery intervals that are relevant to the description of a training programme. At the session level, there is the rest period that is taken between each training repetition or set. This variable can be highly influential in determining the nature of the training programme and will often be closely related to the intensity of the activity. For instance, if the rest period is short, this will limit the intensity of the training as the athlete will not be able to fully recover between each training repetition or set.

The effect of varying the rest period can be profound – completely changing the type of adaptation that is promoted. This can be exemplified by considering a middle distance running interval training session that consists of 6 sets of 200m. If the rest periods are very short (say the length of the interval itself) then this will be a predominantly aerobic challenge and the athlete will not be able to run the intervals at their maximum speed. If the rest periods are around 2 to 3 minutes in length the athlete will be able to run close to their maximum speed, at least for the first couple of repetitions, but they will not have enough time to clear the lactic acid from their system during the rest periods. This session then becomes an anaerobic challenge. Finally, if the rest periods are made much longer (maybe 6-10 minutes) then the athlete will largely be able to recover during the rest period, and each interval can be run close to maximum speed. This final training session is thus a speed or speed endurance stimulus.

The other major rest/recovery interval of importance is the rest that is taken between training sessions. From a GAS perspective, this is clearly a key variable in understanding the subsequent adaptation after training, the relative readiness of the athlete to train again, and the accumulation of any cross-session fatigue. From a practice perspective the amount of recovery between sessions affects how often an athlete can train.

There are a number of other training variables that are sometimes used to describe training programmes that are almost entirely dependent upon the rest/recovery intervals described here (or in conjunction with either the volume and intensity information). For instance, the frequency of training sessions is sometimes listed as a training variable of interest – this is entirely determined by the rest interval between sessions. Similarly, people sometimes talk about the density of a given session – that is, the amount of work done in a particular period of time. Again this is simply dependent on the volume of work performed, the time of the session (another measure of volume) and the amount of rest taken between training repetitions or sets.

3.6. Other training variables

There are all sorts of other variables that can be used to describe a training programme. However, many of them relate to measures of volume, intensity and rest in some way, as seen in the case of frequency and density in the previous section. Even some variables that may not seem to be measures of volume or intensity at first glance might actually boil down to being one or the other on closer inspection. For example, in resistance training people sometimes specify the tempo at which they want each repetition to be performed (e.g. in the bench press spend 2 seconds lowering the barbell to your chest, pause on your chest for 1 second, then spend 2 seconds pressing the weight). The motivation behind this instruction is to increase the amount of time that it takes to perform each repetition – and thus the time that it takes to perform a given set. The reason for this is that the time that a muscle is "under tension" is considered to be a key variable in promoting a hypertrophic response in muscle. However, the time under tension is clearly a variable that describes the volume of training. Thus, although the sets, repetition and tempo guidelines clearly give a very specific description of the training being performed, they largely just describe the way in which volume is accumulated.

3.7. Periodization?

Periodization is really just a fancy way of saying the "planning and organisation of training". This will be a topic that will frequently recur in this book, although I will rarely use the term periodization. People generally invoke the word periodization when they refer to the way in which volume and intensity fluctuate relative to each other over the course of the training year. This fluctuation is driven by the need to ensure that the training performed by the athlete continually provides a stimulus to adaptation - which is the topic of the next chapter.

4 PROGRESSION

4.1. Progressive overload

Progressive overload is probably the most important general guideline for training. As we shall see in a second it is a natural consequence of the GAS theory of training. It is a guideline that is normally associated with resistance training however, it has much wider applicability. The concept was first described in terms of "progressive overload" by DeLorme in the 1940s and 50s[13] however the principle has been well understood for thousands of years. Like a lot of the most profound principles, it is common for people to under-appreciate its importance.

The most famous literary example of progressive overload is the story of Milo and the bull. The story goes something like this. As a boy Milo was given a bull calf. He lifted the calf daily until it was fully grown, and consequently his strength grew to prodigious levels and he went on to have a successful career as a strongman and wrestler. The progressive overload is as follows. The bull calf was small enough that even as a boy Milo could lift it. As time passed the bull's weight increased, creating a stimulus for Milo's strength gain. Because the weight of the bull kept increasing, so did Milo's strength. The stimulus (overload) became (progressively) larger over time.

The justification for progressive overload can easily be derived from a consideration of the GAS. We overload an organism by asking it to perform a demanding task – that is, we apply a stress to the organism, and the organism adapts in a way that accommodates the demands of that stress. In particular, there is an increase in the performance capability associated with the task. If in a subsequent training session the organism is then asked to do exactly the same task it will be easier and thus this time around the stress is less. This in turn means that the stimulus provided by the second training session is smaller. Over time, the adaptation that is caused by performing the task diminishes and progress stalls. Because of the improvements in performance capability, the original task no longer overloads the organism.

From a GAS standpoint, in order to maintain our training improvements we need to ensure that each time we train we overload our body, such that we create an adaptive stress. One way to do this is to use the same task, but to manipulate key training variables like volume and intensity to increase the amount of overload. Most training programmes make extensive use of a limited number of different training modalities, and maybe even a limited number of training tasks, and ensure progression by the manipulation of a limited number of training variables (volume, intensity, rest period, frequency, etc).

4.2. Variety and the cardinal rule of training

One requirement that is frequently described in training manuals is the requirement for variety or variability of training. Again, the rationale for this prescription can be derived from a consideration of the GAS, and is similar to the rationale for progressive overload. We have seen that we will get diminishing returns from our training if we simply keep performing the same task, and that we can counteract this by progressively increasing the physiological load in some way (e.g. by increasing volume or intensity). An alternative way of counteracting the potential diminishing returns is to simply change the task – the new task will challenge the body in a different way and is thus likely to provoke an adaptive level of stress.

Variety therefore seems like a viable strategy to ensure long term improvements. However, there are a couple of major problems. The first is that such a strategy seems likely to violate the cardinal rule of training. If we are constantly switching training tasks are we training with consistency? The second is that we can only change activity if the new activity will stimulate a similar adaptation. The answer to this question is essentially determined by how many potential different tasks there are that might provoke the adaptation in performance capability that we desire. Unfortunately, because in many cases the increases in performance capability that we desire are pretty specific, there are a finite, and to some degree limited, number of tasks available to us.

The guideline for variety in training programmes tends to be satisfied by two means. The first is by changing the training task periodically where possible. The second is by varying the way in which a progressive overload is achieved. For instance, in the first cycle of a training programme progression could be achieved by increasing the volume each week then in the second cycle the progressive overload is achieved by incremental increases in intensity, etc.

As an aside, in powerlifting, a competition that is predicated on lifting as much as you can in the squat, bench and deadlift, there is an approach to training that is particularly creative in satisfying the guideline of variety. This training approach is one of the methods employed at the powerlifting club "Westside Barbell". One effective way in which the body can be stressed is by asking it to provide a maximal performance – for instance, lift the most weight that you can for one repetition. Depending on the task, the athlete's performance level, and their arousal (more on this later in Chapter 14) such a task can be highly stressful, and thus from a GAS perspective might be expected to produce considerable positive adaptations. However, such an approach to training is hard to employ as a long term strategy, as it is hard to provide a progressive overload. The solution that Westside Barbell have found to this problem is to create a whole range of exercises that are similar enough to the competitive lifts to stimulate the desired adaptations, but sufficiently different to stress the body in different ways. By frequently varying these lifts and the nature of the maximal performance (e.g. lift the most weight you can for 1, 3 or 5 repetitions) they are able to consistently stress the body while frequently lifting maximal and near maximal weights in exercises that are very similar to the competitive lifts.

4.3. Minimum effective dose

The concept of the minimum effective dose is another one which is a natural and logical consequence of GAS and is a concept I hinted at in Chapter 1.1. From a GAS standpoint, when we are training we apply a stress that results in an alarm phase, and then the body's response to this alarm phase is to make an adaptation in terms of performance capacity. This in turn prompts a couple of important questions:

- Does a greater stress result in a longer and more severe alarm phase?
- What is the relationship between the length and severity of the alarm phase and the consequent amount of adaptation?

The concept of minimum effective dose emerges if we make the assumption that a greater stress does result in a longer alarm phase, but that any additional adaptation that is a result of this longer alarm phase is not sufficient to compensate for the longer process of adaptation. This then in turn leads to a recommendation that we find the minimum level of stress (dose) that produces an adaptive response and only apply that amount of stress in our training session. This then means that we will recover quicker and our next training session will be sooner. We are thereby able to perform more training sessions within a given period, and thus our overall adaptation is greater. More frequent training sessions are also desirable in terms of the cardinal rule of training.

Although I have posed the concept of the minimum effective dose in terms of the GAS, the concept is clearly consistent with the practice model of training too. The relationship between the difficulty of a practice session and the resulting improvement in performance capability is probably governed by some type of law of diminishing returns. For instance, a 3 hour long practice session won't be 50% more effective than a 2 hour long session. Similarly, we want to practise as frequently as we can. Thus finding the minimum effective dose consists of finding the optimal amount of practice to be performed in terms of the difficulty (volume, intensity, length, etc) of the session and the number of sessions.

A good way of exemplifying the importance of the concept of minimum effective dose is to consider a newcomer to resistance training. A beginner will make substantial improvements even if they train with light loads. Training with heavier loads will be unlikely to result in substantially greater improvement and will just mean that our beginner is sorer and more tired after each training session. Again, we can describe this in terms of the GAS. Because the beginner is unaccustomed to resistance training, even very light activity is likely to result in a stress response as the body has not experienced this type of activity before. It is therefore unnecessary, and quite possibly counterproductive, for the beginner to perform a more intense session.

4.4. "Keeping stuff back"

There is another compelling reason for establishing the minimum effective dose that follows from the limitations of the progressive overload guideline. In particular, we can't just pick a given parameter of the training process and keep increasing it each week and expect to keep improving indefinitely. For instance, if we are training to be as strong as possible in the bench press exercise, we can't simply increase the load that we lift each week by 2.5kg (say) because we will quickly reach a point where we can't actually lift the required weight. We will explore this later in Chapter 8, but unfortunately in progressive overload programmes the rate of progression in loading is normally greater than the rate of improvement in performance capability. However, if we train with the minimum effective dose we will firstly start our training using the smallest amount of overload, and then each week we will progress the overload by the smallest effective increment. This means that we will be able to maximise the returns from whatever mode of training and whatever strategy of overload that we are employing by being able to use that particular training process for longer.

Why might this be desirable? One important reason is that it then allows us to "save" alternative modes of training or loading schemes until a later date – we don't employ them until we really need them. This is clearly a longer term, more sustainable strategy. We try to maximise the improvements that we can make with the current strategy and "keep back" more varied stimuli until later. In doing so we also stay true to the cardinal rule of training – we have more consistency in the way that we are training.

In any particular discipline, "advanced" training methods will exist. In many cases these methods are considered advanced because they are highly stressful. It is very common for people to make the mistake of starting to employ these advanced methods before they need them (this is often either due to boredom or the human desire to innovate, and these threats to the training process are discussed in Chapter 15). In doing so they may "waste" the stressful effect of a novel stimulus by exposing their body to it thereby making it harder to progress later in the training process as they have relatively fewer options of truly novel stimuli to employ.

4.5. The relationship between volume and intensity

So far in this chapter we have seen that the training progress is predicated upon progressively overloading the body. Almost certainly the two most common ways in which this is achieved are through increases in either the volume or intensity of the training performed in a given time period. In many training programmes there is an inverse relationship between volume and intensity – that is, if volume is high, intensity is low and vice versa. The rationale for this is again consistent with some of the ideas discussed in the previous sections. For instance, if in a given period we are seeking progressive overload by increasing volume then it would be overkill to also increase intensity.

The relationship between volume and intensity is described in the most common example of a periodization scheme and is attributed to the Russian sport scientist Matveyev[26] (Figure 4.5). Such a "linear" periodization is very commonly seen in sports where there is just one competitive period. Consideration of Figure 4.5 shows that the progressive overload is first achieved through an increase in volume. Note that in my figure, there is an increase in volume at the start of the period – it is common for volume to be depicted as starting at its highest point – such a scheme would not take advantage of the potential to progressively overload volume in the first place. Following this, volume starts to decrease gradually and there is an accompanying gradual increase in intensity. During this period therefore overload is achieved through moderate increases in intensity while volume is still substantial. Finally, towards the end of the time period when volume is relatively low, overload is primarily driven through more rapid increases in intensity.

Figure 4.5. A typical linear periodization scheme.

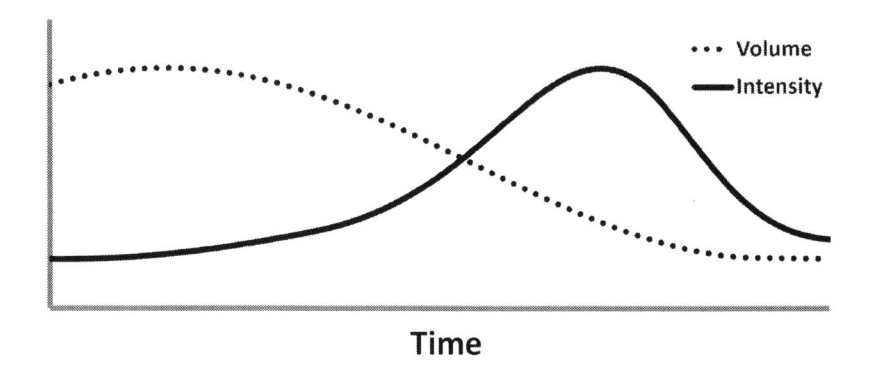

A logical question would be to ask why volume is progressively overloaded prior to intensity. This order is primarily driven by the demands of competition. Typically when we compete we do so at high intensity. It thus makes more sense for the highest intensities of training to be performed near or during the competitive season. This consideration then drives the organization of the rest of the training year.

In his classic book "Supertraining"[34], Mel Siff outlines the volume and intensity combinations typically used by Russian weightlifters. He reports that the most common training combinations are medium to high volume at low intensity (9-10 weeks per year) and medium volume at medium intensity (12-15 weeks per year) – that is much of the training year is spent in the regimes represented on the left hand side and middle parts of Figure 4.5. Conversely, a relatively smaller time is spent training at low volume and high intensity. Of course this is the training practice of just one group of athletes in one sport, but it does illustrate the importance of the relationship between volume and intensity when planning training.

4.6. Progression of training task

As we will see later in this book, we can categorise different training tasks as being more or less "specific" to a particular performance outcome or sport. In its most basic terms, what this means is that some training tasks are more similar to the competitive skills than others (note here that similarity does not exclusively refer to how closely the training task visually resembles the sporting skill). We can use this classification to also ensure that we have a progression in terms of our training tasks across the year.

As in the previous section, the order in which we arrange our exercises is driven by competitive considerations. It makes most sense to perform the training tasks that are most similar to the competitive skill close to or during the competitive period. Consequently we will tend to start the year training with the least specific (most general) training exercises and then progressively employ more specific exercises as we move closer to the competitive period.

4.7. A practice model of progression

So far, the theoretical explanations in this chapter have been heavily biased towards the GAS interpretation of training. How then does practice relate to the ideas about progression that are presented here?

It should be noted that for many sports one of the key training tasks is also the competitive skill (for instance in weightlifting, running or canoeing). In this case it should be noted that when training volume is high, this will also entail a relatively greater amount of practice of the sporting skill. Practice is therefore being "overloaded" by repetition. However, because intensity will tend to be lower when volume is high, the sporting skill is not being executed under the most stressful conditions. This therefore provides an opportunity to focus on technique – using this high volume period to make more substantial technical changes. Conversely, during higher intensity periods of training, practice is more focussed on executing the skill under more competitive conditions. Overload is provided by the intensity of skill execution. The focus of practice then will generally shift to perfecting the expression of force in the skill and/or mental aspects of competitive performance.

5 COMMON TRAINING GUIDELINES

5.1. Introduction

In Chapter 3 we saw how volume and intensity are variables that can be used to describe a training programme. In particular, these are variables that give some measure of the size and nature of the stimulus that is applied by a given training session. The question then arises as to the appropriate stimulus to apply to achieve a given training goal. The purpose of this chapter is therefore to give a brief overview of the guidelines for training that are most frequently seen for a number of common training modalities. As might be expected, these are often posed in terms of volume and intensity.

5.2. Resistance training

Resistance training is the lifting of one's own body and/or external load in order to improve the ability to express force. Classically, weight training guidelines are normally expressed relative to several different training goals (see Figure 5.2.1). It should be noted that these "categories" are not mutually exclusive and there is clearly overlap between each. For instance, if an athlete exclusively trains using "strength" guidelines, we would still

5 COMMON TRAINING GUIDELINES

expect them to increase their overall muscle mass. In fact, only training in one particular category is generally a sub-optimal strategy. To exemplify this, there has recently been a lot of interest in the utility of using more traditionally "strength" based guidelines as an hypertrophy strategy.

Figure 5.2.1. Typical resistance training guidelines (table adapted from Sheppard and Triplett[22]).

Physical Quality	Intensity (%1RM)	Repetitions per Set
Strength	≥85%	≤6
Power	75-90%	1-5
Hypertrophy	67-85%	6-12
Muscular Endurance	≤67%	≥12

Figure 5.2.1 presents a very typical summary of the most common weight training guidelines. The inverse relationship between volume and intensity that was described in Chapter 4.5 is clearly evident: for example, strength training is characterised by higher intensities (weight used) but lower volumes (less repetitions per set).

General guidelines such as those seen in Figure 5.2.1 have considerable utility but can be misleading for credulous readers. Probably the most problematic guideline is the suggestion that to train for increases in strength it is necessary to use a load that is ≥ 85% of your 1RM. This seems to suggest that unless you are training at this intensity you will not get stronger, and can lead people to try and consistently train at this intensity. Such an approach would be very hard, both physically and mentally, and as we shall see later will probably not lead to optimal strength improvements.

Figure 5.2.2 presents the average yearly training intensity of elite Russian weightlifters. It can be seen that the average intensity of squatting performed by these athletes is between 60 and 70%. If these numbers are interpreted in light of Figure 5.2.1 it would suggest that these athletes spend most of their time training for hypertrophy. Such a suggestion is clearly incorrect – weightlifting is a weight categorised sport and so generally elite athletes will not want to get bigger, however they will want to get stronger while staying at the same body weight.

Figure 5.2.2. Average training intensity of elite Russian weightlifters. Figure adapted from Medvedyev[27].

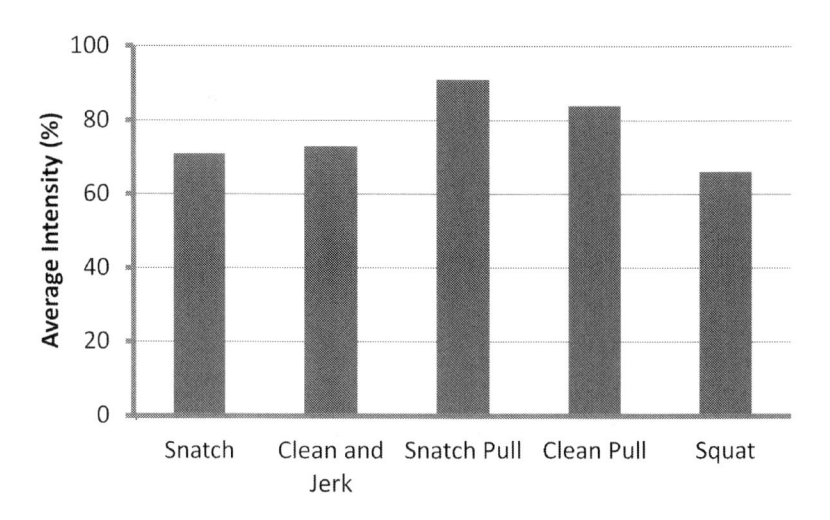

How can we explain this apparent contradiction between Figures 5.2.1 and 5.2.2? It's actually not easy, and it is probably easier to understand where it arises from. Tables such as the one in Figure 5.2.1 tend to be derived from peer reviewed scientific literature. Amongst the well known weaknesses of this research is that the duration of such studies are relatively short (maybe 8-12 weeks). It may well be that intensities of 85% or greater yield better results in a one-off intervention over this type of time period. However, this does not suggest that such an intensity is optimal in the long term – and one of the key messages of this book is that it probably isn't.

It is interesting to note that the most famous Russian weightlifting guidelines don't stipulate a given range for strength or hypertrophy training but rather just the volume and intensity relationship (Figure 5.2.3). They also stipulate a maximum number of total repetitions to be performed.

Figure 5.2.3. Prilepin's Table indicating the optimal repetition ranges for the Olympic weightlifting classical lifts to be performed at a given intensity. Table adapted from Medvedyev[27].

% of Maximum	Number of Repetitions Per Set	Total Lifts
70	3-6	18
80	2-4	15
90	1-2	10

5.3. Endurance training

Similar to resistance training, typical guidelines for endurance training tend to specify a variety of different training zones, and then lay out the intensity of training required to be within each zone. Due to the simplicity of measuring heart rate, intensity is often described in terms of heart rate zones. For the general population these zones are somewhat generic – the only subject specific information that is used to specify the zones is the person's maximal heart rate, which in turn might be estimated from their age. However, for elite athletes detailed physiological testing can be performed to try and match heart rate zones to different energy production regimes as described briefly in Chapter 3.4.

Figure 5.3.1 depicts some typical heart rate training zones that are commonly used by Great Britain Rowing. Although these zones specify the intensity of exercise, they don't provide prescriptions for how this is achieved, the volume of training or how it is structured. As would probably be expected, lower intensity exercise is often performed at higher volumes. Often this is continuous "steady state" activity that is performed at the same intensity. In contrast, the higher intensity zones can only be reached during interval training – that is bursts of high intensity activity punctuated by rest periods.

Figure 5.3.1. Typical rowing heart rate training zones (adapted from GB Men's Rowing Team Guidelines[19] and the FISA Training Program for Clubs and Individuals[28])

Heart Rate Training Zone	Intensity (%MHR)	Blood Lactate (mmol/l)
Fuel Utilisation (UT3)	<59	<1
Basic Oxygen Utilisation (UT2)	59-67	<2
Oxygen Utilisation (UT1)	67-75	2-4
Anaerobic Threshold (AT)	75-85	≈4
Oxygen Transport (TR)	85-95	4-8
Anaerobic Capacity (AC)	95-100	>8

An alternative way in which to describe endurance training sessions which gives some of the detail of the volume and structure of the session is by stipulating the ratio between periods of work and rest (Figure 5.3.2). However, in this case the intensity of the activity could vary widely within each category dependent on the effort exerted by the athlete.

Figure 5.3.2. Energy system contribution for different work to rest ratios (adapted from Bowers and Fox[10]).

Primary Energy System	Interval Duration (s)	Work to Rest Ratio
Stored ATP & Creatine Phosphate	5-10	1:12 to 1:20
Anaerobic	15-30	1:3 to 1:5
Anaerobic & Aerobic	60-180	1:3 to 1:4
Aerobic	>180	1:1 to 1:3

What is important to note here is that these guidelines give little guidance as to how different types of endurance training sessions should be combined in order to reach a particular endurance goal.

5.4. Speed, agility and plyometrics

Common guidelines for speed, agility and plyometric training don't tend to be posed as formally as those for resistance or endurance training. However, they still tend to be described in terms of volume and intensity. However, for these qualities training guidelines are less focussed on the type of adaptation that is being promoted and more on simply minimising injury risk by limiting the volume of training. Probably the most common ways of quantifying volume for these activities is either in terms of distance covered or number of foot contacts. For speed and agility training, intensity is often not stipulated – the assumption is that each repetition is performed with maximal effort.

Plyometrics are exercises that are designed to increase force expression abilities, generally by using impact loading and the body's reflex response to this in order to promote high rate of force development and peak forces. These exercises often consist of jumping and bouncing movements. Again, volume guidelines are typically given in terms of total foot contacts. In terms of intensity, exercises are classified as low, medium or high intensity, and then the number of foot contacts is determined based upon the intensity of activity. Unusually, plyometric training guidelines do often provide some type of indication as to how volume and intensity are progressed as athletes improve their level of qualification.

5.5. Flexibility

Guidelines for flexibility and mobility training are also pretty sparse. In terms of static stretching intensity is normally stipulated in terms of the perceived level of pain (e.g. "stretch until a point of mild discomfort") whereas volume is generally specified by time. A common guideline is to hold a stretch for 10 to 30 seconds and then maybe to repeat the stretch. There are 2 principal ways in which stretching can promote improvements in flexibility. The first, which is probably the mechanism which is most intuitively easy to understand, is by changing the physical properties of tendons, muscles and ligaments making them more elastic. The second is by training the nervous system to be more relaxed in extended positions. Again, although acute guidelines for flexibility training exist it is very rare to find any recommendations on how flexibility training should be structured in the longer term.

5.6. Guidelines for progression?

General guidelines for training such as the guidelines that have been presented in this chapter tend to have 2 notable omissions. The first is that it is often unclear what should be the initial starting level in terms of volume and intensity prescription for athletes of various levels of qualification. The second is that the rate of progression in terms of either volume or intensity is often not defined.

When trying to establish an appropriate starting point a good guideline is to err on the side of doing too little, rather than too much. In effect, choosing the right starting point is a question of establishing the minimum effective dose. Starting too light is not generally a problem – it is easy to increase intensity of volume over the next couple of weeks to reach an optimal level, and "losing" a couple of weeks training in this way is unlikely to be that serious (in fact, a gentle run in to a new training programme is probably a good idea). However, most people when starting a training programme will tend to go the other way – performing gruelling sessions that leave them tired and sore. Such an approach means that from the word go the adaptive capacity of the body is severely challenged, and it is more difficult to progress the loading of the activity.

The question of rate of progression and the structure of training generally is more complicated to answer, which may be why this is so absent from the common guidelines. I will cover this in detail over the course of the next 3 chapters.

6 THE STRUCTURE OF TRAINING

6.1. What is the purpose of the training unit?

In this chapter we will start to look at how training can be most optimally organised. Before we can do that however, we need to have something to organise – a training unit. A training unit is simply any given bout or bouts of training that we designate as one "block" based on some useful criteria. In practice we will most often designate a training unit as being a particular training session (the criterion here simply being that it is the discrete period of time that you spend being sweaty). However, sometimes it might be helpful to designate a particular group of exercises within a training session as being one training unit due to similarities in the type of activity or the goal.

In order to most optimally organise our training units we need to be able to characterise their purpose. In accordance with the theoretical background of this book described in Chapter 1, at the highest level it is useful to label a training unit as either a tangible or intangible unit, based upon the nature of the adaptation being sought:

- A tangible unit will be one that is more influenced by GAS considerations and that will be relatively more focussed on making tangible adaptations;

- An intangible unit will be one that is more influenced by the practice model of training and that will be relatively more focussed on making intangible adaptations.

I must again stress that it is not my intent to suggest here that a tangible unit cannot promote intangible adaptations and vice versa. Of course, any training unit will be likely to cause a plethora of both tangible and intangible adaptations. Instead this method of classification is based upon being clear as to the purpose of the training unit – are you trying to impose a stress on the athlete which will provoke an alarm phase, or are you simply practising? When put in these terms:

- A tangible unit will likely be of higher intensity or volume and in many cases will produce higher levels of fatigue;
- An intangible unit will be focussed on the skilful performance of movement, and will often produce lower levels of fatigue.

Earlier in this book I argued that the dominant training paradigm was GAS based. This is manifested by the fact that many training programmes will contain many tangible training units and few intangible units. I believe that most people would benefit from having many more intangible units within their training programme.

6.2. Freshness and fatigue

Another way of categorising training units that is often useful is in terms of their freshness requirements and the fatigue they cause. To elaborate, some training units require you to be very fresh in order to perform them properly, whereas others can be completed when you are tired. Similarly, some training units will cause high levels of fatigue, whereas for others the fatigue implications will be modest. We can therefore categorise training units according to a matrix like the one in Figure 6.2.

Figure 6.2. Classifying training units based on freshness and fatigue qualities.

Fatigue Qualities

Freshness Requirements	High	Low
High		
Low		

The characteristics of each quadrant and some examples are as follows:

- High freshness/high fatigue: these will often be units that require an athlete to work at high intensity. The athlete needs to be fresh in order to access this intensity. Similarly, having worked at such an intensity they are likely to be tired, even if the volume of the session was quite modest. Examples might be maximum strength training or speed endurance sessions;
- High freshness/low fatigue; these sessions require the athlete to exhibit high levels of concentration, velocity or acceleration, but that may be lower in volume. A good example might be an agility training session, or a distance runner performing "strides";
- Low freshness/high fatigue: these are units which do not require much intensity, effort, concentration, velocity or acceleration, but that may be of higher volume. A classic example would be a basic hypertrophy session (i.e. one that is aimed at building muscle). There are lots of repetitions to perform, but these can still be performed if the athlete is tired from other training;
- Low freshness/low fatigue: these are sessions that the athlete can still perform productively when tired, and that won't create huge amounts of fatigue. Examples might be some types of technical practice, recovery sessions, core training or stretching.

The organisation of a training programme and in particular a training week, then becomes an exercise of scheduling an athlete's training units such that they are fresh for the training which requires it. Of course, this clearly requires some training units to be prioritised and compromises made, as it is unlikely that the freshness requirements will be able to be met for all training units.

6.3. Pareto's Principle

Vilfredo Pareto was a 19th century Italian economist. He is perhaps best known for the 80/20 rule that is named after him and which has application in a number of fields. For instance, in business the rule suggests that 20% of a company's customers will account for 80% of its income. Pareto's Principle is sometimes used to describe training programmes hence its appearance in this book. In this context the principle would tell us that just 20% of the training we perform will create 80% of the improvements in performance capability that arise from a training programme.

Clearly what is important when considering Pareto's Principle is not the exact figures describing the relationship (i.e. is it 80/20, 70/30, 80/30 etc) but rather the spirit of the principle. That is that a relatively small amount of the training that you do each week will account for most of your improvements.

If we accept the fact that a relatively small amount of our weekly training programme will account for most of our improvements, this leads to a number of implications. Clearly it is highly important that we know which parts of our training programme are the ones that account for the most significant improvements in performance capability (which from this point forward I will refer to as the "hot sessions"). This then allows us to prioritise these training sessions, as follows:

- First and foremost, our priority is to make sure that each week we perform the hot sessions. If our training time in a week is limited, we will generally ensure that at the minimum we complete the hot sessions;
- It is important that we are fresh enough to be able to train optimally during the hot sessions, and this consideration becomes a key driver in our organisation of the training week;

- All of the other sessions that we do, aside from the hot sessions, only account for 20% of our improvements. We thus need to be careful that we don't fall into the trap of overestimating the importance of these other sessions.

We should also recognise that the specific figures describing Pareto's Principle will vary depending on the goal of the training programme and the training philosophy of the person writing the training programme. For instance, one key training outcome for a marathon runner might simply be to accrue a certain amount of running mileage per week. In this case the 80% of training (which I will refer to as "everything else") represents the bulk of the weekly mileage and might account for a greater proportion of the improvement in performance capacity. Conversely, a powerlifter might be able to make considerable progress training only 2 or 3 times a week. In this case, the training programme really only consists of the hot sessions, and there isn't much everything else.

The ideas presented in this chapter can be succinctly encapsulated by proposing two corollaries to Pareto's Principle:

Pareto's Principle: "20% of your training (the hot sessions) will account for 80% of your performance improvements."

=>

Corollary 1: "Make sure you perform the hot sessions, and that they are completed with the most optimal quality."

=>

Corollary 2: "Don't do things that affect your ability to perform the hot sessions with optimal quality."

6.4. The number one error

It is my firm conviction that the most common error that people make in training is that they violate the second corollary of Pareto's Principle. That is, it is very common that people train in a way that prejudices their ability to perform the hot sessions with high quality. The reason for this is that it is common for people to wildly overestimate the importance of everything else. Such a mistake is a consequence of the common belief that one should always give "110%" in training. This belief then leads an athlete to train with high effort and/or high intensity in every training session. Consequently, when it comes to the hot sessions, the athlete is too fatigued to be able to perform the sessions with the most optimal quality.

It is therefore very common that athletes perform most of their training sessions at similar levels of intensity. This is often even true when the athlete is aware of the hot sessions and understands that they should be of higher intensity. A classic example of this is the training of the overzealous distance runner. As we shall see shortly, in a typical distance running training programme, there will be 2 or 3 hot sessions that are run at higher intensities (e.g. intervals run on the track, or sustained running at a challenging pace). The rest of the training week will consist of regular training runs aimed at accumulating mileage. The overzealous distance runner will want to work hard during these training runs and complete them at a moderate intensity, which in turn means that they are not fresh when it comes to the hot sessions and can only complete them at a moderately high intensity[4]. In contrast, the second corollary of Pareto's Principle would dictate that the bulk of the weekly mileage should be run at low intensity if this is what is necessary to be able to complete the hot sessions with high or maximal intensity.

The behaviour that I have typified using the example of the "overzealous distance runner" is prevalent across the training spectrum. It is very common that athletes perform most of their training at a moderately high intensity and there is not much variation in the intensity of their training across a training week or a training cycle. This is because many athletes are not prepared to train at lighter intensities as this is insulting to their work ethic, which in turn means that they are rarely fresh enough to train at the highest intensities.

Many people think that an important role of the coach is to encourage, motivate and exhort an athlete to work hard in a session. My view is almost the opposite of this. I have found that most competitive athletes are quite prepared to work hard as described above. Instead, often the role of the coach is to hold an athlete back – to make sure that they are not working harder than they should, particularly when training everything else. Of course, sometimes the coach needs to encourage athletes to work hard, but this is normally in providing support to help an athlete work hard when they want to (e.g. providing loud vocal support if an athlete is trying to work near to maximum intensity) rather than pushing an athlete to do something they don't want to.

6.5. How does Pareto's Principle relate to training theory?

How can we explain Pareto's Principle in terms of the training theory that we discussed in Chapter 1? This is challenging, however it is possible to make some generalizations that I think are helpful. In particular, I think it is useful to compare Pareto's Principle to the two different models of training that I contrasted earlier.

Firstly, we have the GAS, whereby we stress the body sufficiently to put it into an alarm phase, and then allow time for recovery and compensation. If we were to strictly adhere to the principles implied by GAS, the length of time associated with this stress – recovery cycle, would mean that we can only have a limited number of training sessions in a week. For this reason, in many cases it is most appropriate to think of the hot sessions as seeking performance improvements based predominantly on GAS type adaptive mechanisms. That is, these sessions tend to be the more stressful ones, and hence they tend to provoke greater adaptations (this is why they are the important ones). The reasons why such sessions might be stressful can vary – for instance they could be of high volume or high intensity or both.

On the other hand, we have also talked about a practice model of adaptation. This seems to be the mechanism by which everything else might work. We don't want to train in such a way that we compromise our ability to recover from the hot sessions. However, this doesn't preclude us from performing some lower intensity/lower volume/low fatigue activities. That is, we can do lots of low-fatigue practice while we are recovering. In fact, as we will see later, some of this practice activity might even help us to recover, and is also important in providing the base for the hot sessions to be effective.

Of course, it's important to recognise that the above broad brush picture of adaptive mechanisms is a gross generalization, and that there will be an element of crossover. For instance, if a weightlifter performs maximum attempts at the competitive lifts as part of a hot session there are clearly GAS and practice elements. On the one hand these attempts will be highly stressful for the central nervous system and likely be a powerful stimulus towards strength improvements. However, the weightlifter is also rehearsing the actual competitive performance i.e. practising. Similarly, a middle distance runner will often perform a number of short "easy" runs over the course of a week. These can be characterised as practice, but will probably still promote adaptations that improve aerobic performance. (As an aside, the mechanism of this cannot be easily explained by the theory that was previously presented, which suggests that we are still some distance from a complete description of the mechanisms of adaptation to training).

6.6. Structure of the training week

Pareto's Principle and its corollaries provide us with some very clear guidelines for structuring the training week, that are consistent with the theory of training that was presented earlier in this book, and the concepts of freshness and fatigue that appeared earlier in this chapter. When we sit down to plan our training week, the first thing that we need to do is identify our hot sessions. We then schedule these in the most optimal places in the training week. We then organise all of the other training sessions around the hot sessions, first making sure that we will be fresh enough to perform the hot sessions with high quality, and then trying to find the best place to perform the rest of the sessions taking into account their freshness and fatigue qualities. Of key importance is the fact that many of the training sessions should have low fatigue qualities.

It is exceedingly likely that as we start to put our training week together that we find that we aren't fresh as often as we would like. This is a natural consequence of the fact that for many training sessions it is most optimal to perform them when we are fresh. Often this will not be possible for all training units, and so we will need to make compromises. Some training sessions will often need to be performed under some fatigue, even if this is not optimal. Deciding which sessions we need to be fresh for is a key question and should be based on an understanding of the sport and the athlete's needs (see Chapter 10).

6.7. An example: the training week of a mile runner

In this chapter we shall deconstruct the (winter) training week of a mile runner. The training week needs to include the components listed in Figure 6.7.1. (hot sessions in bold). Note that some aspects of training (e.g. flexibility training) are omitted for clarity.

Figure 6.7.1. Classification of the training units of a middle distance runner.

<u>Fatigue Qualities</u>

Freshness Requirements	High	Low
High	• **5 x 1 mile (2 mins recovery)** • **30 minutes at lactate threshold**	• Strides (fast running over short distances)
Low	• **Long run (80 mins)** • 2 x strength training	• 7 x easy runs (20-35 mins) • Core training • Running drills and hurdles

6 THE STRUCTURE OF TRAINING

The structure of the training week is then as depicted in Figure 6.7.2.

Figure 6.7.2. The middle distance runner's training week.

	AM	PM
Monday	Easy run then running drills	Easy run
Tuesday	Strides + 5 × 1 mile	Strength training
Wednesday	Easy run	Easy run
Thursday	Strides + 30 mins threshold	Strength training
Friday	Easy run then running drills	Easy run
Saturday	Long run (80 mins)	Core training
Sunday	Easy run	Rest

In analysing the above training week we should first look at the position of the hot sessions. In particular, note that in the day preceding each hot session the athlete only performs easy running, in order to maximise their freshness the following day. Of the hot sessions, the interval training session on Tuesday demands the greatest freshness, and consequently there are 2 days of lighter activity preceding it. The long run, which will be fatiguing, but does not require the athlete to be as fresh (it is just work, that is not performed at a particularly fast speed), comes towards the end of the training week when the athlete will be more tired.

In the above plan, strength training is performed on the same day as the hot sessions. This will seem counter-intuitive to many coaches who would consider that strength training should be performed when fresh in order that an athlete can perform the training with high quality in order to reap the most benefits. However, for the mile runner the most important components of training are the high quality running sessions and they need to reserve their freshness for this. In addition, the strength training sessions will tend to be quite fatiguing – thus they are placed after the hot sessions so that the fatiguing sessions are grouped together and the recovery between them can be maximised. Of course, this does mean the quality of the strength training will be compromised as the athlete will already be fatigued, however this is an acceptable compromise given the focus of the training programme.

Finally, it is also worth noting that the most frequent activity is easy running. This is both practice and recovery.

6.8. The fractal structure of training

I'll start this section with full disclosure up front. I'm pretty sure that all of the ideas here are stolen directly from a lecture that I heard Dan John give a few years ago.

In this chapter of the book we have spent quite a long time talking about the structure of the training week. We have not, and will not spend anywhere near as much time talking about the structure of a training session, a training day, a training month or a training year. This is because a lot of the ideas that have been presented in this chapter are directly applicable to each of these time intervals. The reason for this is that, as Dan John has observed, training programmes tend to have a somewhat fractal structure.

What is a fractal structure? A fractal image is an abstract pattern that has the property of "evolving symmetry" (see Figure 6.8). What this means is that if you zoom in to a specific region of the image you will find a pattern that is similar to the whole. If you then zoom in again you will find another similar image, and so on.

6 THE STRUCTURE OF TRAINING

Figure 6.8. A section of the Mandelbrot set – a famous example of a fractal image. The image was created by Wolfgang Beyer using the programme Ultra Fractal 3 and is reproduced here under the terms of the Creative Commons Share Alike 3.0 license.

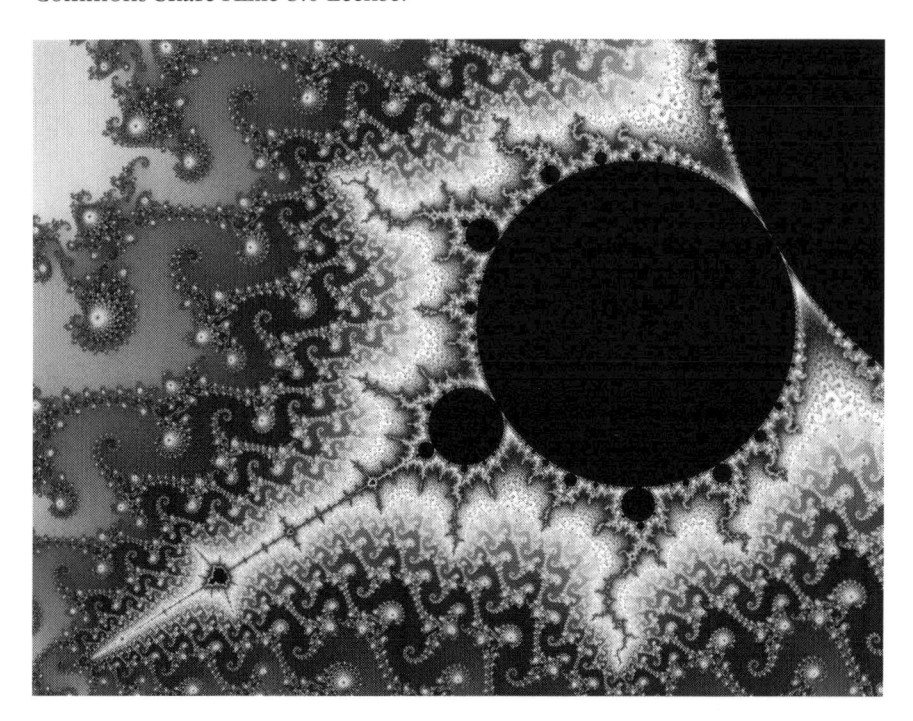

We can describe training as having a fractal structure as it also has this property of being similar if viewed from different scales. For instance, if we look at a training week we can see that there is a pattern of hot sessions and practice sessions and that these are ordered to try and optimise freshness and fatigue. If we then "zoom in" to look at a particular training session we can see a similar pattern. There will be "hot exercises" that are the most important aspects of the session (the 20%). There will be exercises that are very fatiguing but that don't require high amounts of freshness. There will be practice exercises. All of these will be organised to try and manage freshness and fatigue within the session.

Similarly if we "zoom out" to the level of the annual plan we might also see a similar structure. There will be training cycles that are of very high intensity and/or very specific to the sporting goals of the athlete that represent the "hot cycles". There might be periods of over-reaching where a lot of work is performed generating large amounts of fatigue, but the quality of that work is not necessarily that high. There will be periods of recovery and of practice.

Of course, there are specific considerations that apply to the structure of these different training time intervals just as for many fractals the pattern within a pattern is similar but not the same. However, one can get a long way towards writing a complete effective training plan by simply applying the concepts described in this chapter of the book.

7 BUILDING A BASE

7.1. Introduction

In Chapter 6 we started talking about the structure of training, mainly focussing on the structure of the training week. In the next two chapters we will look at the two main structural aspects of training programmes when considered over multiple weeks.

In this chapter I will talk about training to build a foundation. In order to exemplify the concepts under discussion I will show how they apply to the training of a rower. However, the same ideas are readily applicable to almost all other training goals.

7.2. Building performance capability

In the next two chapters we will look at how performance capability is "built". The building metaphor is apt as high level performance training largely consists of two aspects. The first is the establishment of an extensive training base. This then acts as the foundation for the second aspect - subsequently higher intensity training and competition. Most people probably have some intuitive understanding of what we mean by a training base, but it is worth reviewing this.

Probably the most common context where people might refer to a training base is in endurance sports like rowing. In Chapter 2.3 we saw that there are 3 major systems that provide the energy for movement and that generally all are engaged to some degree in any activity. This then raises the question as to which energy systems should be trained when, and the training strategy that should be employed for each. The most common solution to this dilemma is to treat the aerobic energy system as the "base", and then to use this as a platform for developing the anaerobic energy systems. There are a number of good reasons for the focus on an aerobic base:

- The anaerobic system is dependent on the aerobic base as both a determinant of the intensity at which anaerobic energy production is required and for the processing of some of the products of anaerobic metabolism;
- Competition will generally involve the greatest involvement of the anaerobic system (for instance, rowing as competed at Olympics and World Championships is really a middle-distance sport with a substantial anaerobic component). Thus a sensible organisation of training relative to the competition period is to focus on anaerobic system training closer to competition – this necessarily means that aerobic focussed training comes earlier;
- Because the aerobic system provides energy at lower intensities and for longer durations it can be activated and trained with lower intensity/higher volume activity. Higher volume training will again tend to come earlier in a season. Similarly, training the aerobic system predominantly with lower intensity training means that higher intensity training sessions can be saved for anaerobic training sessions.

From the example of aerobic base above we can make some general characterisation of what base training is. Base training will often be focussed on physical capabilities that are important for the performance of the sport and that underpin the most specific capabilities, but that may not be the most direct determinants of performance themselves. There will be an emphasis on base training early in the season (and early in an athlete's career), and base training will often be driven by higher volume and higher frequency approaches.

The second aspect of building performance capability is building up from the base and will be the subject of the next chapter. As when building any structure, the success of the project depends on the base. The wider and more extensive the base, the higher we can build.

7.3. The "tank"

What are we doing when we build a base? One common metaphor that is used to describe base building is to "expand the tank". This emerges from the English expression of "having nothing left in the tank" – that is that you are exhausted. In this expression, we are comparing our body's energy reserves to the fuel tank of a vehicle, and suggesting that when we are exhausted we have no fuel left. When used in this context, emptying the "tank" is an acute effect – once we have rested and recovered we would expect to replenish our fuel reserves (refill the tank).

The concept of expanding the tank is a helpful metaphor to understand base building. If we build a big tank then we will have lots of fuel available to support other training activities. Another metaphor for base building is to build a big engine. In this case the metaphor suggests that we have a lot of brute horsepower (think tractor) but that this will need to be refined later for performance purposes (think race car).

If we return to our example of a rower, then the building of an aerobic base comprises lots of volume of lower intensity activity that is performed earlier in the season in order to support later more specific activities. They are seeking to expand their tank through tangible physiological adaptations that will improve the delivery of oxygen to their muscles and the ability of the muscles to use this oxygen to release energy. In base training they are making an investment in their future training and competition performances.

Although this discussion has used rowing as an illustrative example of the meaning of the tank, it is important to recognise that the concept has utility across training domains. For instance, in Olympic style weightlifting it is common to talk about an athlete's base strength. This could refer to several things, but might often relate to their leg strength. Similarly, in lifting sports the concept of work capacity (Chapter 2.3) relates to how much total training an athlete can perform. Training to improve either of the above two qualities can also be characterised as expanding the tank – a base is built that is then used to support more specific, higher intensity training.

7.4. The problem with Pareto

In Chapter 6.3 I introduced Pareto's Principle – that is the principle that (approximately) 20% of an athlete's training will account for (approximately) 80% of the improvement in performance capability. However, there is an important caveat to the application of Pareto's Principle to guide and understand training which relates to the concept of base building. This caveat is as follows: Pareto's Principle is highly applicable in the short term, but requires some modification when it is applied in the long term.

Pareto's Principle would seem to imply that an athlete could actually eliminate 80% of the training that they perform and still expect to enjoy most of the improvements in performance capability by just performing the hot sessions. In the short term, this interpretation of Pareto's Principle is probably true, however in the medium to long term the gains in performance would dry up if employing such an approach. Although the "everything else" of training may not be the direct primary driver of large improvements in performance capability in the short term, the establishment, maintenance and growth of a base of training is a necessary pre-requisite for continuing improvements that are driven by the more intense training.

Perhaps a helpful analogy to understand this is to return to the economic roots of Pareto's Principle. Remember that when Pareto's Principle is applied to business it suggests that a business will generate 80% of its income from 20% of its customers. However, it would not be a viable strategy for a business to divert all of its resources into working with the most profitable 20%. Over time, this 20% would erode – for instance, as customers moved to other suppliers or went out of business. It is important that the business keep working with its other customers and keep marketing to expand its customer base, especially as some of these customers will ultimately graduate to being in the most important 20%.

7.5. Greasing the groove/filling the tank

So far, the discussion in this chapter has mainly been implicitly posed in terms of tangible adaptations. For example, the rower builds an aerobic base by performing high volume training which results in tangible adaptations that improve her aerobic capacity. These imply a GAS based mechanism of adaptation. Similarly, the description of base building has been focussed on higher volume, general training that is performed towards the start of a competitive season. However, in Chapter 6 we saw that the bulk of the training week consists of lighter sessions that are not GAS focused. Instead these are used for base building and maintenance. To understand how this works it is helpful to consider base building in practice terms.

When we practise our aim is to improve our ability to execute a skill. This is easy to understand if someone is learning a skill, or if we have a measurable outcome (e.g. a basketball player who makes an increased percentage of their free throws). We can also understand how practice can help an elite performer refine the aspects of their technique which are visually apparent. However, there is a benefit to practice that is more intangible, and that I refer to here as "greasing the groove". Imagine rolling a cricket ball along a dirty drain pipe. If you repeat this motion over and over, then with time the ball will remove the debris from the pipe and the ball will run more smoothly. Once the pipe is clean if you then lubricated the pipe the ball would roll even more smoothly. This is what we are doing when we repeatedly practise the skill, eliminating tiny flaws, improving fluency and getting better at expressing force without wasting effort.

When we practise at sub-maximal intensities we are trying to make the skill feel as effortless as possible. In doing so, we aim to bring up our base. In other words, if something is easier than it was before, then it implies that we have improved. These improvements in our base should transfer into improvements in maximal performance, especially if they are also supported by higher intensity work in the hot sessions.

Of course, repeated lower intensity practice of skills almost certainly can result in tangible adaptations too. For instance, consider the physique of male gymnasts who build extensive musculature simply by practising the skills of their sport. This adaptation is very difficult to explain using a GAS based model.

7.6. Leave the session feeling better than when you started

So in most cases the bulk of an athlete's training sessions during a week should be predominantly practice orientated. This means that during the course of the session the athlete should improve their skill at the activity, while trying to minimise the fatigue experienced. If this is achieved then the athlete should leave the session feeling better than when they started. That is, the net effect of the positive improvement in skill minus the negative effect of fatigue should itself be positive – they should have improved their performance capability (and probably their body and mind should feel better).

This description of leaving a session feeling better than when you started probably sounds very alien to most people. In all probability, for most people, the outcome of a training session is almost always tiredness. However, I would suggest that actually, in most cases, a training programme should consist of many more feel good sessions than feel bad sessions.

7.7. What is a recovery session?

Although the idea of many practice sessions might seem like a departure from traditional ideas around training, the concept of a recovery session is not. Recovery sessions are based on the premise that the adaptation and recovery of an athlete from training can be enhanced by performing physical activity – that is recovery will be faster as compared to just resting. However, again, the traditional explanation as to how recovery sessions work is based upon a consideration of tangible adaptations. For instance, the runner who goes for an easy jog in the afternoon following an intense morning track session facilitates their recovery by encouraging the circulation of more blood, helping remove the waste products from the intense session and bringing nutrients to aid adaption. Or alternatively, a rugby player who goes in the pool the day after a game aids their recovery by restoring their mobility.

There are some practice based explanations for the effectiveness of recovery sessions too though and I think they are generally more compelling than the traditional ones. If an athlete performs a high intensity/high volume GAS focussed session then it is likely that, at least towards the end of the session, their technical execution of the skills begins to break down. They are thus practising a sub-optimal version of the skill. Similarly, the effect of these less than perfect repetitions is probably greater than for normal practice repetitions, given the fact that the mind and body of the athlete is so engaged in the session, and due to the strength of the adaptive response that is likely to follow. In this model of a recovery session the athlete uses the practice session to recover the skill that their high intensity training has degraded. If we take the example of our rower, in their intense GAS based session they may have rowed with poorer form, reverting to old habits or compensations as they fatigued, and undoing some of the technical progress they may have recently made.

Alternatively, the importance of a recovery or practice session may be in ensuring that any gains in capacity that result from the GAS based session are incorporated within the athlete's new performance capability. For instance, following an intense GAS based strength training session our rower will be creating new muscle tissue and laying down new neural pathways (etc etc). If they practise well during this adaptation period this may influence the nature of the final adaptation. Similarly, after the athlete has fully recovered from a GAS based session and has an elevated level of capacity, it is then important to practise the skill to ensure that the new capacities can be expressed during the skill.

Of course, it is likely that both tangible and intangible mechanisms explain the effectiveness of recovery sessions. However, I do believe that most fundamentally, maintaining form by doing feel good practice sessions is more effective than complete rest.

7.8. How does this apply to strength training?

I think that most people would argue that the most important skill that is expressed during strength training is the ability to express maximum force (a more thoughtful coach or athlete might add the requirement that the activity should also be performed with good technique). I don't. Instead, I think the most interesting skill that is derived from strength training is the ability to move a sub-maximal weight (let's say between 70 and 90% of 1RM) fast with good technique.

Given this definition of the skill involved in strength training, it is then easier to understand how practice sessions can improve performance capability. We don't need to be lifting at high intensity or with high volume to get better at moving a sub-maximal weight fast. Similarly, it is easier to see how one can improve their skill during the course of a session – as the athlete greases the groove they will become more efficient with their movement, performing the lift faster, whereas the relatively lighter weight and absence of fatigue allows them to work on technique.

One aim of a practice session therefore becomes to make a given load move as fast as possible, with the best possible technique, and with the lowest perception of effort. As an aside, if the athlete is successful in improving, there will likely be a benefit to their top end strength too. For instance, if 80% starts to feel like 75%, both in terms of speed and effort, then at least part of this improvement is likely to be due to an increased maximum. (Note that the reason I say a part is that one desirable adaptation to strength training is that the athlete is also able to move quicker with a greater relative load. Thus the other part of the adaptation will simply be that the athlete is able to move faster with 80% of their new maximum).

Recovery sessions are particularly important based on this interpretation. Firstly, if an athlete performs a higher intensity session, they may compromise their technique and so this needs to be restored. However more importantly, maximal and near maximal efforts, or the final repetitions in a set that approaches failure, will tend to be slow. The athlete will grind out the lift, and "grindy" lifts are very far from the skill that we are trying to encourage. It is therefore particularly important that the athlete gets back in the gym soon and remodels a fast and proficient lift.

7.9. Autoregulation

Autoregulation is a training strategy that is based upon allowing the athlete (or the athlete's performance) to determine the difficulty of a training session based upon their freshness – this is sometimes called their readiness to train. Autoregulation is often contrasted against an approach whereby the difficulty of a session is dictated to an athlete – for instance by stipulating the volume or intensity. Either approach can be employed in base building.

Personally, for me the practice approach to base building is generally most effective if it is autoregulatory. Remember the purpose of our session is to improve our skill or form during the session, in order to feel better at the end of the session. We thus need to pick an intensity of training that is easy enough to allow us to practise well – this will be determined by our freshness. We can then increase our intensity in line with improvements in our form across the session, however we must make sure that our perception of effort is appropriate for the session. If the session is supposed to be easy we should not increase the intensity to a point when it is not easy. Similarly, there are autoregulatory constraints on the volume of our training. Certainly we should stop training if further practice will decrease our form. Sometimes we will practise until our form stops improving. At other times we might continuing practising once we have reached our peak level of skill for the session in order to grease the groove of that improved technique. Often we will stop practising before we start to fatigue unless some fatigue is a desired training stimulus, or we have a lot of recovery time prior to the next session.

7.10. Examples

As we saw in Chapter 6, in middle distance training the athletes perform a lot of easy running – this is the key practice activity throughout the year. However, there are other aspects to their practice. In particular, the middle distance runner needs to make sure that they keep practising running fast throughout the year. Perennial tissue conditioning activities are important and are often performed in the weight room and through the performance of running drills. In winter months there will be an emphasis on base building of both aerobic capacity and strength/muscular work capacity. I will provide a little more detail on the variation in a middle distance runner's training across the season in Chapter 11.6.

The foundational base of weightlifting is strength in squatting and pulling. Depending on the abilities of the athlete this foundation is important enough that it can often be a focus of the hot sessions. Certainly, the weightlifter will always have an eye on this base, and will grease the groove in the squats and pulls frequently. For a weightlifter, practice is comprised of technical practice in the competitive lifts and their derivatives. Speed of movement is emphasised at all times, and especially in practice. Other lighter base building activities involve increasing work capacity and tissue conditioning/hypertrophy.

8 BUILDING UP

8.1. Introduction

In Chapter 7 we saw that one important aspect of a training programme is the establishment of a solid base and its maintenance. This chapter will describe the other main aspect of a training programme which is the increase in the performance demands of training throughout the training cycle. As in the previous chapter I will draw on a recurring example in order to exemplify the discussion. In this case we will consider training to improve bench press performance.

8.2. The practical application of progressive overload

In Chapter 4.1 I introduced the key concept of progressive overload. One thing that many successful training programmes have in common is the degree to which they are governed by this concept. Similarly, although progressive overload was first posed as an idea that applied to resistance training, it has wide utility across a range of training modes.

To recap, the idea behind progressive overload is simple. In training we perform some activity that acts as a stimulus to adaptation. In GAS terms we apply a stress that creates an alarm response and that the body then adapts to. However, if we then perform the same activity in the same way the stimulus to adaptation is weaker. Again, from a GAS perspective, the fact that we have adapted means that the second training session provokes less of a stress response and so the consequent adaptation is less great. In order to keep improving we need to make the training activity more challenging. In doing so we ensure that we still induce a stress response despite the fact that our body is now capable of a greater level of performance. We make the training activity more challenging by increasing the volume of training, its intensity, or by manipulating any number of other parameters. The point is that we need to progress.

It should be noted that one aspect of the base building described in the previous chapter can be interpreted as an application of progressive overload – that is, in each week we try to increase the amount of work that we perform. In this context, we progress in terms of the weekly volume. However, often when we are base building we are not seeking an overload stimulus in terms of the base building activity and so we don't target a high level of fatigue due to very high weekly volumes (one exception being if we are over-reaching).

Employing progressive overload as a strategy for training is astonishingly effective provided certain conditions are met. It is possible to realise a very great increase in performance capability after only a few weeks training. For this reason, progressive overload is frequently the determining factor that is used for programming the week to week progression of the hot exercises and sessions.

8.3. Rate of progression

So we have established that we need to employ progressive overload within our training programme! But what should this look like? For instance, a common resistance training recommendation within the fitness industry is that you should train with a load that you can lift for (say) 8 repetitions. Once you are able to lift that load for 10 repetitions (i.e. 2 additional repetitions) you should then increase the load slightly and repeat the training programme. This is clearly progressive overload – once your strength has increased by a given amount the absolute load lifted is increased. Is this the most optimal way to implement a progressive overload programme though?

To answer this question, let's consider a concrete example. Let's say that my maximal bench press performance is to lift 100kg for 8 repetitions and that my training programme consists of doing one set of 8 repetitions. From GAS considerations, my training session is a stress that causes an alarm phase which I then adapt to. Thus when I am fully recovered and come to do the same training session in the following week I am stronger – let's say I could now do 9 repetitions with 100kg. My criterion for progression is that I need to be able to perform 10 repetitions with 100kg before I can increase the load, thus I stick at 100kg for my training session in week 2. However, because I am now stronger, performing 8 repetitions with 100kg is sub-maximal and not as stressful. The consequent alarm phase following this training session is less severe, and thus my adaptation less great. Let's say that following recovery my capacity is to now to be able to lift 9½ repetitions (!). Again, this is less than the required 10 repetitions so I perform training session 3 with the same load, and this time around the stimulus is even less, and so on.

Thus what we see is that this method of progressive overload will actually result in diminishing returns each week that you train with the same load. This argument will apply whenever we use exactly the same loading (in terms of volume and intensity or anything else) in consecutive sessions with full recovery – in the second training bout the stimulus for adaptation will be less.

What if our criterion for progression was that once we were strong enough to perform just one additional repetition (i.e. 9 repetitions) we were able to increase the weight? In this case, we would be permitted to increase the load in our second training session. Let's say we increased the weight to 102.5kg which (coincidentally) was our new 8 repetition maximum. Now our second training session would involve the application of a very similar relative training stress – in both weeks 1 and 2 we perform one maximal set lifting the most weight we can for 8 repetitions.

This then seems to suggest a more optimal strategy for progressive overload. Each week, all we need to do is to increase the loading by exactly the amount that represents the improvement in performance capacity that we have made since the previous training session. This will then mean that the stimulus we apply each week is then kept constant relative to our performance capability – we progress the loading in such a way that the difficulty relative to our capability is the same. Clearly this is not something that is possible to do however. We need to test our strength to know the improvement in performance capability, but testing our strength requires us to perform the activity, and performing the activity is training that will change our strength level. Similarly, it is not really possible to exactly quantify the improvement in strength. Finally, the contention that this method is most optimal is based on the assumption that training at 100% of 1RM provides the same stimulus from week to week provided that the 1RM is adjusted to reflect improvements in strength. This is also probably not true – we will grow accustomed to lifting maximally, and over time this will become a less stressful activity even if the relative intensity remains the same.

We have seen therefore that from a progressive overload perspective it is not optimal to use the same load from session to session. Instead, we need to increase the load in some way. We have just seen that although it could be optimal to increase the load in a way that reflects our improvement in performance capability, such an improvement is not practically achievable. We are thus left with the choice between increasing the load by either more or less than our relative improvement in performance capability.

If we were to increase the load each week by less than our improvement in performance capability then the relative stress that we apply to our body will be smaller than in the previous week. Consequently we would expect a smaller increase in performance capability after the second week's training. This loading strategy therefore results in diminishing returns in a similar way to using the same load each session, just at a slower rate, and at some point our improvement will plateau. We are thus left with the recommendation that we want to match our increment in load to our improvement in performance capability, but accepting that this is not realistic, we want to err on the side of increasing our loading by more than our improvement.

8.4. Wave loading

Our argument in the last section led to the recommendation that our rate of progression when building up should be greater than our improvements in performance capability. However, this leads to a problem as well. If we increase the load by more than our improvement in performance capability then we will ultimately reach a point where we have increased the loading to a point where we can't actually complete the programmed session. This then means that we can't continue to employ the same progressive overload strategy. How then can we continue to progress? One option would be to simply change the training task, or the method of progressive overload (e.g. switch from volume driven to intensity driven). This is a viable strategy, but does restrict our training options.

Fortunately there is another solution to this problem. If we considerably reduce the loading to a level that is only slightly higher than the level at which we originally started the progression then we find that we can then run a similar progression and get similar results. Effectively the body seems to "reset" in terms of its adaptive response.

Figure 8.5 (in the next section) presents a visual depiction of how this type of progressive overload looks in practice. This strategy is most often referred to as "wave" loading, because each cycle of progression looks a little like a wave. The reason why wave loading works is challenging to explain simply in terms of isolated repeated applications of the GAS. In the next section I will propose a mechanism to explain why the strategy works and then I will use this theory to discuss recommendations for wave loading, and why they are effective.

8.5. Adaptive capacity

In Chapter 8.3 I asked whether if we were able to exactly match our loading increment to our increase in performance capability that we might simply be able to keep progressing in this way forever. In fact this isn't the case. Continuing with our bench press example, consider a training programme where each week we simply lift as much as we can for one repetition. This type of training programme can be pretty effective, but only for a very limited period. If we were able to increment the weight of the bench by sufficiently small amounts, we could arguably get close to matching our improvement to our loading increment. However, even in this scenario, we get diminishing returns. This is difficult to explain based on an isolated consideration of the GAS alone – if we are applying the same stimulus relative to our increased strength then we should be stressing the body equally. This should lead to the same adaptation. Thus provided we are getting adequate recovery why don't we continue improving forever?

The answer to this apparent contradiction lies in the fact that we can't view each application of a stressful stimulus in isolation. The body "remembers" its history in some way, and even if the same relative stimulus is applied the response is not the same. There are two likely mechanisms for this:

- The body becomes accustomed to the type of stress being applied. Thus even if the same relative loading is applied, the body does not find it so stressful and the alarm phase is less deep. This in turn results in a smaller adaptation (Figure 8.5a);
- The body has a finite ability to adapt. Thus even if the second alarm phase is equally as deep the body is not able to compensate as much as it did after the first stimulus (Figure 8.5b).

We can encapsulate both of these ideas within the same model if we introduce the concept of an "adaptive capacity." When the body is recovering from and adapting to a training stimulus it uses some adaptive capacity. This is then replenished when the adaptation is completed (Figure 8.5c). If the adaptive capacity is high then the body will be more sensitive to training stimuli and/or exhibit a greater degree of adaptation to a given stimulus.

As can be seen in Figure 8.5, it is easy to find situations where the performance capability is fully recovered but the adaptive capacity is not. If a training stimulus is applied before the adaptive capacity is recovered, then the training programme results in a progressive decrease in adaptive capacity.

Figure 8.5. Diminishing adaptive capacity results in diminishing improvements in performance capability. See text for description.

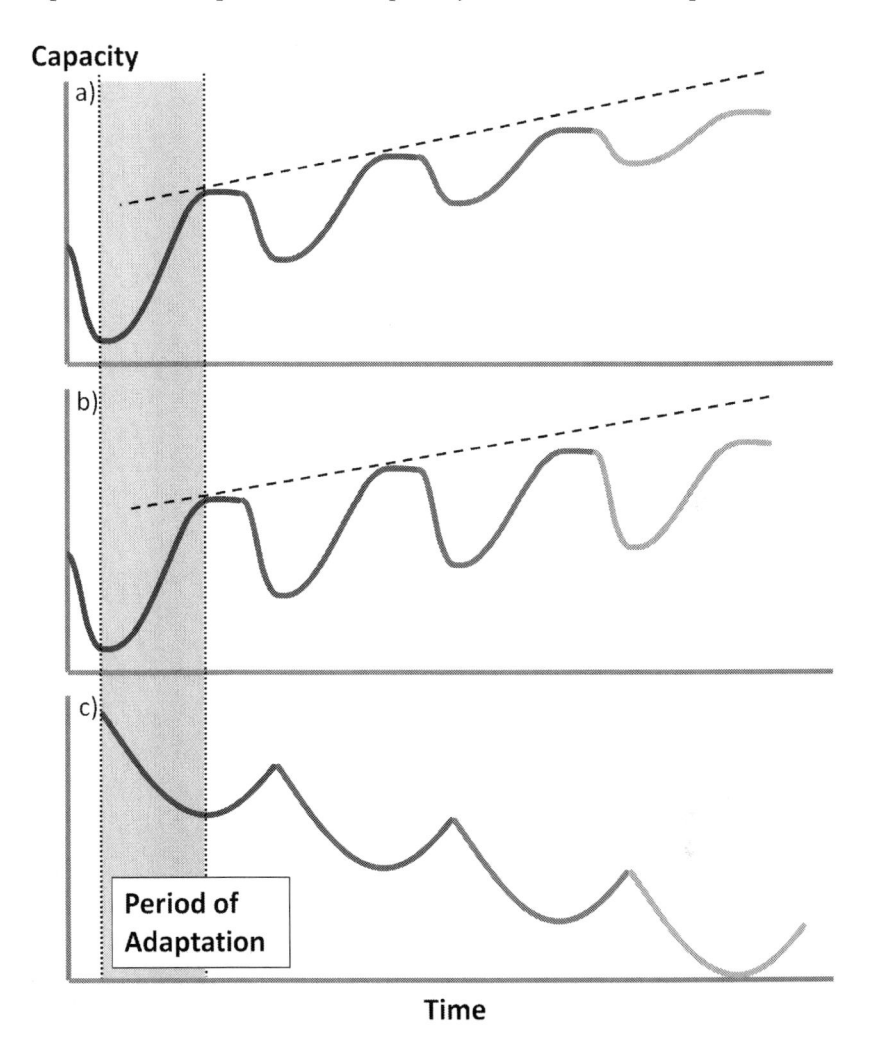

What is the practical impact as adaptive capacity decreases? Essentially as we go through a cycle of progressive overload it becomes harder to make further improvements. In order to keep an optimal rate of improvement we either need to increase the relative size of our stimulus (i.e. to increase the loading faster than our gain in performance capability) and/or accept that as we go through the cycle our improvements will necessarily wane (although not by as much as they would if we did not increase the loading).

How does all of this theory explain the fact that wave loading works and in particular the fact that the body "resets" at the start of a new wave? When we reach the end of a wave this does not mean that all of the loads that we used during the wave are now too low or light to cause an adaptive response, relative to our performance capability. It is just that they are too low/light to cause an adaptive response relative to our adaptive capacity. If we then reduce the loading (or rest) it allows our adaptive capacity to be fully replenished and then we are able to run a new wave.

It is worth commenting on the meaning of this concept of adaptive capacity. I am not suggesting that this is a "thing" within the body. Rather this is a proposed model that helps us in understanding, explaining and maybe predicting the response of the body to training. Philosophically it doesn't matter if the model actually represents the reality, only if it is useful. Another example of a model used in sports science is the spring-mass model that is used to describe running[7] – a spring with a weight on top does not resemble a person, but it does give good predictions of running behaviour.

8.6. A practice based explanation of wave loading

The above justification of wave loading was posed in terms of the GAS however, there is also a practice based explanation. The easiest way to envisage this is to return to our bench press example, and to consider what we mean by "skill" in bench pressing. Clearly at the most fundamental level skill in bench pressing is simply the ability to express force within the lift. However, I would contend that there are other important aspects to the skill, which can provide a practice based explanation for the efficacy of wave loading. In particular, skilful bench pressing also includes the ability to perform the lift with perfect technique and to move the barbell with high velocity (at least with sub-maximal loads).

Let's assume that at the start of the wave we have reached a high level of skill in bench pressing. At the start of the first wave, where the loading level will be reasonably modest, we will be able to exhibit this skill – we will perform the required repetitions at speed and with good technique. However, as we increase the loading across cycles, the training load will progressively get closer to our maximum. It is likely therefore that the technical excellence with which we perform the repetitions will start to decrease. Similarly, at the heavier loads we will move the barbell with less velocity. Thus as we progress through a cycle we effectively practise a sub-optimal version of the skill.

As we approach the end of a wave our skills and capacities within the bench press have changed. We will have improved some aspects of the capacity that is our ability to express force, for instance in increasing the amount of muscle tissue we have or our neuromuscular system's ability to recruit muscle. However, at the same time some of the finer aspects of our skill will have decreased. We reach a point therefore where we need to take a break from increasing our bench press brute strength, and instead practise the skill of bench pressing in order to best incorporate our higher levels of strength.

Clearly, the start of a new wave provides a perfect opportunity for skill practice. We reduce the weight such that the performance of each repetition is relatively easy. We can thus focus on technique and bar speed. Over the course of the first couple of weeks within the new wave we recover our bench press skill, incorporating our gains in strength capacity. This will therefore account for the improvements in performance capability that we might see in the early parts of the wave, and provide a platform for further improvements in capacity later in the cycle.

In order to pose the practice model of wave loading in more general terms we can characterise it as follows. As we build through a wave we increase our capacity in some physical quality, however at the same time some aspects of our skill might wane (or at least do not increase). Therefore, the early part of the subsequent wave is a period of transformation – we improve our skill levels in order to incorporate our enhanced capacity.

Again, it is important that when we consider the above explanation we remember that "skills" and "capacities" are somewhat arbitrary categories. For instance, there are skill/intangible aspects to the increases in strength capacity we build throughout a wave, and these are not entirely distinct from the skill increases that we might work on at the start of a wave. However, there are substantial differences in the character of the activity at the start and end of a wave.

8.7. Start light

So far in this chapter I have argued that wave loading is one of the most effective ways to "build up" and have presented some ideas on the most optimal rate of progression. However, what we haven't considered so far is the starting point for the wave – i.e. what should be the level of loading in week 1? This is a critical issue to the success of a wave loading protocol, and one that many people get wrong. Why should we start light? Well, starting light is consistent with the concepts of minimum effective dose and "keeping stuff back" that were described in Chapter 4, and as we shall see these recommendations are important in wave loading.

When we implement a wave loading protocol the idea is that we increase the loading over a period of weeks. The amount of adaptation that we should expect will be modest. For instance, considering our bench press example, if we were to increase our maximum by 5kg over the course of 6 weeks we would be ecstatic. If we start our wave progression close to the maximal load that we are currently able to handle then the length of the wave will be short – even taking into account an increase in strength we will quickly reach a level where we can't achieve the programmed session. Thus, in order to have a wave of optimal length we need to start relatively light in order to have a period of a number of weeks before we reach our current maximum.

Similarly, we have already seen that as our adaptive capacity diminishes over the course of a wave we will need to use progressively greater relative loadings. We thus need to start with a light relative loading (minimum effective dose) such that we can subsequently increase the loading. This is the reason why a training programme that consists of lifting your maximum each week isn't effective – although the absolute loading increases it is not possible to increase the relative loading across the cycle. We need to start light and hold something back such that we are able to progress the difficulty of the session across the cycle.

Finally, in the previous section we saw that the early part of a given wave is also practice focussed. For instance, in our bench press example we would be using the early part of the wave to work on technical excellence and speed of execution. In order to meaningfully practise these aspects of a skill we need to use a lighter load.

There is a convincing evidence base for the efficacy of starting light comprising both practical experience and research. For instance, the maxim to start light is an important aspect of some of the internet's most popular strength training programmes (e.g. Jim Wendler's 5/3/1[36] or the Stronglifts 5x5[21] programme). Similarly, a student of mine studied wave loading for the bench press as his Master's dissertation and found that starting light is at least as effective as starting heavier[38]. Despite this, it is often very hard for a person to force themselves to train light enough in the early part of a cycle. We will return to this issue later in the book.

8.8. The problem with peaks

As we have seen in this chapter, building up is a very successful and widely employed strategy in training. However, there is an important caveat to its use – that is, that we shouldn't be too greedy about the gains that we try and make in a given wave. Many people stunt their improvement by seeking too much of an improvement too quickly. The easiest way to understand this is to observe that from a training perspective (not a performance perspective) there is a fundamental problem with a peak. If you reach a peak that implies that after reaching a high level of performance capability, your capability then falls substantially (Figure 8.8.1).

8 BUILDING UP

Figure 8.8.1. The other side of the training peak. Image of the mountain designated CC0 by www.maxpixel.net.

Pointing out the fact that the realisation of a peak implies a subsequent decrease in performance capacity may seem like a semantic argument, and some readers may be sceptical about the significance of such a subsequent drop. In reality, the drop in performance after a "true" peak can be very large. The reason for this is relatively easy to understand if we consider the concept of adaptive capacity that was introduced in Chapter 8.5. If we are really to reach the highest peak in performance capability that is possible, we will seek to maximise every shred of our adaptive capacity. A consequence of this is that following this peak we will need to rest for a considerable amount of time in order to recover our adaptive capacity. During this period of rest our performance capability will wane. Similarly, in order to realise a training peak, we will often also devote less time to the maintenance of our foundation – effectively we start to empty the tank in order to achieve our peak.

The combination of a reduced adaptive capacity and an empty tank could conceivably explain the very large degree of "drop off" that can occur after realising a peak. However, we can also speculate about the existence of a further mechanism.

So far in this chapter we have used the concept of adaptive capacity to describe the potential of the body to improve its performance capability above the baseline level, and have assumed that our ability to recover to our baseline level is unaffected by our prior training. Such an assumption could be questioned, as there is almost certainly a crossover between adaptive and recovery processes. Thus, as our adaptive capacity decreases it probably also compromises our ability to recover. How can we include this factor within our model of the training process?

One way is to make an arbitrary theoretical distinction between adaptive and non-adaptive recovery processes. Non-adaptive recovery processes we define to be things like the replenishment of energy stores or rest to eliminate neural fatigue. Adaptive processes could be things like the repair of exercise induced muscle damage. If we describe the training process in these terms, then we can show the adaptive and non-adaptive processes (Figure 8.8.2). In Figure 8.8.2 even recovering to our baseline level requires some adaptation. Thus such a model suggests that if we achieve a peak, and entirely deplete our adaptive capacity then we won't even be able to recover fully from training. In this case if we continue to exercise and/or train then our performance capability will reduce.

Figure 8.8.2. Response to stress in terms of adaption (including adaptive recovery) and non-adaptive recovery processes.

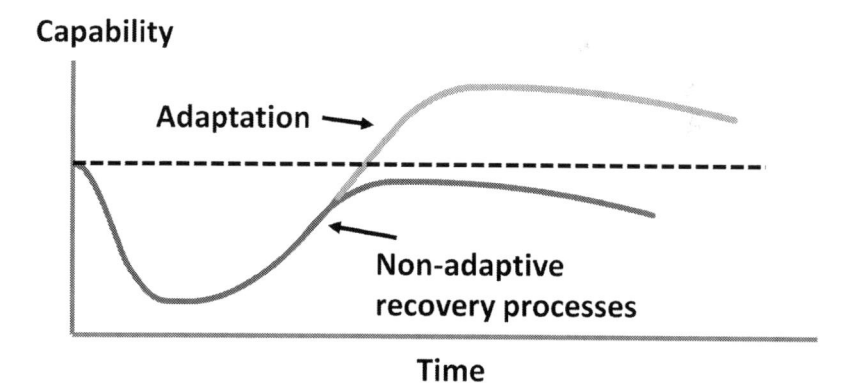

8.9. How long is a cycle?

In the previous section I described a fundamental limitation of wave loading – that is that if we achieve a peak in performance capability we would then expect a considerable depression. Such a pattern of progression would not be optimal in terms of long term performance improvements. In particular, our performance capability will vary greatly over the course of a year, and we will infrequently be near our peak performance capability.

In fact, it is quite common for athletes to exhibit such a pattern in their training, especially in the lifting sports of weightlifting and powerlifting. This is partially due to the popularity of "specialization" programmes that are readily available and which are designed to quickly increase your capacity in a given physical quality. For instance, there are a large number of squat programmes that promise to "improve your squat by 25 pounds in 6 weeks" or similar – for instance the Smolov Squat programme[35], Russian squat generator (actually the Zeinalov squat programme[40]) or the Maslaev squat programme[14]. The problem with such programmes is that they tend to be highly demanding – an athlete does increase their squat capacity during the programme, but in doing so runs down their adaptive capacity. It is thus very common that a handful of weeks after finishing the programme their squat is essentially back to where it started.

Of course, it is fine to build to a peak if the peak is planned to coincide with a competition, and there is plenty of time to build up again prior to the next competition. However, in order to assure the best long term progression you would only want to use this type of strategy sporadically. Similarly, if the quality that you are training is a general quality that you need as an athlete (as squat strength tends to be) or if you have frequent competitions you certainly don't want to build to a peak and then suffer the consequent decrement in performance.

A much more viable long term strategy is to be more circumspect in the goals you set yourself for a given cycle. In particular, you should be modest in the amount of improvement you target in a particular cycle. If you progress too fast you will use too much adaptive capacity, not to mention the increase in injury risk.

Most descriptions of wave loading tend to based on the idea of starting a new wave when you are no longer improving. In contrast, I would contend that the best way to "build up" using wave loading is to shorten the length of the waves by starting a new wave before you reach the peak of the current wave. In doing so, you skip the end of the wave which is characterised by training relatively hard to realise only small further increases in performance capability. Instead, once you have reaped the larger performance gains from the start and middle of the wave you drop down and start a new wave.

> "Start light and progress slowly."

8.10. Burying yourself

To this point in this book I have been emphasising the fact that most people train too hard too often. I have advocated starting light and have suggested that it might often not be strictly necessary to train at maximum intensity. At this point therefore I think it is important to clarify that I am not suggesting that doing gruelling sessions is inappropriate. Of course these very definitely have a place in the training process. However, more often than not the primary rationale for their inclusion is not for the adaptive stimulus, even though, as we have seen, maximal efforts can provide a very profound stimulus. Instead, maximal efforts or punishing workouts tend to be valuable in developing competitive skills and/or the mentality of the athlete.

Many sports require the expression of maximal intensity efforts and thus the need to practise these is a no brainer. Similarly, in very many competitive environments the ability to tolerate pain is a huge competitive advantage. These qualities need to be developed in training.

The training practices of some athletes are sometimes hard to justify based purely on the adaptive stimulus for physical improvements that is being applied. The volume and intensity of activity is sometimes far in excess of what would be required based simply on the principle of progressive overload. However, the athlete needs to learn how to tolerate that level of pain in order to develop the toughness and bravery that is required to be successful. However, at the same time, it is common for athletes to make the mistake of thinking that they need to train in this way all the time in order to develop toughness. This is not true – toughness can be developed with far fewer hard sessions than most athletes think.

8.11. Autoregulation

As for base building, autoregulation is also an important strategy in building up, but is deployed in a different way. Often when building up it is useful to plan how the progression will look in terms of the volume and intensity of the hot sessions across the cycle. It is possible to leave this to an athlete's feel, however it requires a great deal of self-discipline to hold oneself back appropriately in the early part of a cycle if intensity is not stipulated. By and large therefore, the athlete will know the target for the session, and because they should be adequately fresh for the session it should be realistic to expect they will achieve it.

Where autoregulation plays a role in building up is in judging the length of a particular cycle. We need to adjust the length of the cycle based upon the ease with which the athlete is adapting to the programme and progressing. If a particular progressive overload strategy is still producing improvements we generally want to keep going (within the constraints of the competitive programme and the annual plan). Similarly, if the improvements of the athlete start to stall, we don't want to keep plugging away week on week, putting in a lot of effort during training but making minimal gains.

8.12. Examples

As was the case in the previous chapter, I will close this chapter with a couple of examples of how building up can look in practice. I will just focus on building up towards a competition here, but as we have seen, building up is a strategy that should be used across the training year.

One approach to building up to a 1500m race is to perform sessions that become increasingly closer to the actual event, particularly in terms of the speed of running. There are various ways to do this. For instance, one "set" in a session could be something like 800m, rest, 300m, rest, 400m. The total distance covered in the set is 1500m. The athlete can perform multiple sets separated by longer recovery periods. This set can easily be manipulated to make it more intense (and closer to the competitive challenge) by increasing the pace at which the intervals are run, and by decreasing the rest periods between the intervals in a set. A very specific session that is performed the week before a race might involve running the intervals at race pace with only 30-45s between them.

I have chosen to present just one session here, and shown how it can be manipulated across several weeks to increase the intensity and specificity of the activity. This is for clarity, however in practice middle distance runners tend to perform different sessions from week to week. However, the clever coach can ensure that the physiological demands of the sessions are intensified in the desired way by manipulating the distance, pace, recovery and volume of the session. It is also important to note that building up to a fast 1500m is achieved across various fronts. For instance, race pace isn't the peak running velocity that is targeted – the athlete will also build up in terms of faster running too (above race pace).

In powerlifting training it is very common to build up towards a competition in a very traditional way (increasing intensity, decreasing volume). One interesting wrinkle in powerlifting is that it is competed in "equipment" – tight reinforced clothing that can considerably increase the loads lifted. As the athlete builds to a competition they also have to practise the skill of using the equipment most effectively. This needs to be incorporated into the progression. I will show how this is done for the squat.

A typical competition cycle in powerlifting might be 12 weeks, split into 3 smaller cycles. In the first cycle the athlete might build up "raw" (without equipment), in the second cycle they might add knee wraps, and then in the third cycle they also include the squat suit. Across each mini cycle, the load lifted increases while the volume decreases. One approach is simply to try and hit a given "top set" each week. This might be a set of 5 in week 1, 3 in week 2, a double in week 3 and then a heavy single in week 4. This pattern is then repeated across each cycle – as the equipment is incorporated the weight lifted jumps substantially. So for instance, across twelve weeks the top set might look something like the following (all weights in kg):

- Weeks 1-4 (raw): 5 @ 170, 3 @ 180, 2 @ 190, 1 @ 200;

- Weeks 5-8 (knee wraps): 5 @ 190, 3 @ 200, 2 @ 210, 1 @ 220;

- Weeks 9-12 (equipped): 5 @ 210, 3 @ 220, 2 @ 230, 1 @ 240.

9 LEARNING SKILLS

9.1. Introduction

In the last 6 chapters the discussion has mainly focussed on training to improve capacities. However, as we saw in Chapter 2, training to improve performance capability also involves the learning and refining of skills. In this chapter I will therefore offer some brief thoughts on skill learning. Again, in the interests of full disclosure I should make it clear that many of the ideas here come almost directly from my great friend Jon Goodwin.

The learning of skills is often described in terms of some type of hierarchy of mastery[15]. At the most novice level skills require a great deal of conscious control, reducing their fluency. As an athlete becomes more skilled, the skill will start to become more automatic, with less conscious processing required. However, at an intermediate level performance of the skill might be disrupted if the demands of the task are increased. At the highest level of mastery the athlete will exhibit fluid automatic performance that is resistant to disruption even under competitive stress.

In the skill acquisition literature it is also common to make a distinction between "closed" and "open" skills. A closed skill is one where the athlete does not have to react to the external environment, for instance in Olympic style weightlifting or the throwing events of track and field. In contrast, an open skill is one where the athlete has to adjust the skill in response to some external stimuli – for instance in team sports like football, basketball and rugby. Some sports have a mix of closed and open skills - for example, in tennis the serve is a closed skill (weather aside) whereas the rest of the rally is open.

One fascinating aspect of motor control is that skilled performance is not uniform with no variation from one repetition to the next. The seminal work in this area was performed by Nikolai Bernstein[5] who studied the way in which expert blacksmiths used their hammer, and who found that there was a great deal of variation in the trajectory of the hammer. In skilled performers there are aspects of the skill that are stable and that are consistently displayed in each repetition whereas there can be considerable variability in other aspects of the skill. In contrast when a novice performs the skill there won't be a distinction between the stable and variable aspects – there will just be variation across the board. It is thought that the reason for this "good" variability is that it allows a skilled performer to adapt to the changing demands of the competitive environment.

9.2. General to specific skill learning

As we shall see in the next 2 chapters, it is common to categorise training activities on a continuum from general to specific, where general activities tend to improve a person's overall athletic ability whereas specific activities are tightly focussed on improving capacities employed in the sport in question. Performance capability can be enhanced by improving in either general or specific regimes. We can view skill learning in a similar way.

It is my belief that the ability to learn skills is trainable. To perform a new skill, the brain has to learn a new way of coordinating the body. The more skills an athlete knows, the better they are at moving. This ability will then be reflected in a capacity to perform new movements easily, not least as the athlete may be able to adapt skills that they already know to the new task. This is one of the reasons why there can be great benefit in athletes performing activities that are very far removed from their competitive environment.

9.3. Repetition and drilling

Clearly in order to learn a skill practice is required, and generally to perfect a skill will require a large number of repetitions. The appropriate way in which to "drill" a sequence of skills is a topic that has received quite a bit of attention within the academic literature. In particular, 2 different approaches to practice are generally described – blocked and random practice[25]. Blocked practice is where the same skill is repeated multiple times prior to moving on to the next skill to be practised. For example, a tennis player hits 100 backhand drives, then 100 forehand drives, etc. As might be expected this leads to the quickest short term changes (improvements?) in a skill. In random practice the different skills that are being practised are interspersed among each other – for the tennis player whether they hit a forehand or a backhand is randomised. The advantage of random practice is that changes to the skill are retained for longer.

9.4. Thinking is bad

As we have seen, a typical pathway for the learning of a skill begins with the athlete consciously controlling themselves (thinking), but then with increased mastery the skill becomes automatic. Trying to consciously control yourself through a skill is generally bad – conscious control of movement is slow and clunky, whereas automatic control is fluid and fast. Despite this fact, it is common for athletes to work very hard (in their mind) to execute a skill perfectly. This behaviour can seriously retard the learning process as the athlete is preventing themselves from executing the skill automatically. A good example of this is in Olympic style weightlifting - a ballistic movement that should be performed with the intent to move quickly. A common mistake that beginners make is to concentrate on making sure that they hit various key body positions during the course of the lift – this focus then changes the whole character of the lift, making it a controlled movement rather than a "throw" of the barbell upwards.

Moreover, in some skills there is very limited time in which to think – for instance in jumping or throwing. An athlete who relies on a strategy of

9 LEARNING SKILLS

thinking through the skill performance will be hampered in their ability to learn the skill.

Similarly, some skills are reflexive in their nature. Jon Goodwin illustrates this perfectly by asking a group of athletes to race over a short distance (say 15m). The starting position of the athletes should be standing upright with their feet parallel to each other. The quickest way to start from this position is to first split the feet – moving one forwards and one backwards simultaneously. This is the quickest strategy as it is the quickest way to get into the optimal start position (some people disagree and call this a false step – they are wrong). When given the instruction "go" all of the athletes will automatically perform this movement and then start accelerating. In fact, it is actually really difficult not to perform this movement – even if you strongly encourage athletes to not take the false step, they will still take it on multiple occasions provided that they are still being encouraged to race as fast as they can (and this will be accompanied by lots of frustration and hilarity). When the athlete finally manages to start without a false step it will be slow, both because the strategy is inefficient, but also because the athlete has to wrench control of starting from their sub-conscious and there is a long pause as they think.

Another mistake that coaches sometimes make is to feel that they need to teach these reflexive skills. Thus they will demonstrate the split, and then get athletes to drill it. Aside from the fact that this is unnecessary as everyone knows how to split, it also makes the athlete slower. Instead of using their reflexive, fast skill they instead bring splitting under conscious control.

9.5. Constraints based learning

How do we teach or learn skills like those described above without hampering the development of automaticity or the use of reflexes? The answer to this lies in allowing an athlete to use what they already have or in challenging them to figure out the skill for themselves. It is important to emphasise that in this context "figuring out" does not mean by thinking but by trying. In the case of skills where the athlete likely has an existing reflexive strategy we just need to set up some type of activity that challenges them to use it, and then practise. We can add rules or physical challenges (constraints) to the activity in order to nudge the athlete towards more skilful movement.

In the case of more complex skills constraints are also useful. In this case, the constraints may be more rigid (literally or figuratively) but will guide the athlete to the appropriate strategy. For instance, in the example of Olympic weightlifting that was given earlier a good constraint is to emphasise to the athlete that their knees should be back when the bar passes the knee (Figure 9.5). For many athletes if this happens, then the other aspects of the skill tend to fall into place.

Figure 9.5. Knees back as the bar passes the knee in Olympic weightlifting.

The use of the term "constraints" can be confusing, as it seems to imply that there is a physical object or presence that governs performance of the task. This is a misunderstanding. The constraint can be something as simple as ensuring that the athlete begins the movement from a particular starting position. Similarly, verbal cues are a constraint – if an athlete is cued strongly to make sure that they exhibit a particular behaviour (e.g. knees back in weightlifting) then this is a constraint to their movement.

> "In movement coaching, verbal feedback IS a constraint. It's not something outside the constraints led process. We just need to pay attention to how it modifies the athlete's behaviour. Nudge the athlete, don't control the athlete."
>
> Tweeted by Jon Goodwin, 14th May 2018

The purpose of the constraints is therefore to create an environment for the athlete to experiment with movement in such a way that they can find their own optimal way of performing the skill. Using the term "constraints based learning" to describe this type of exploratory approach to learning is somewhat of a misnomer, as more traditional, instructional approaches to coaching and learning are also constraints based. What is different is the nature of the constraints and their purpose. In instructional approaches the athlete is supposed to try and faithfully execute each aspect of the skill in the way that is dictated by the instructions whereas in exploratory approaches the constraints are designed to encourage the non-negotiable (stable) aspects of a skill while giving the athlete freedom to experiment in areas where variation is desirable.

> "Talk to athletes about shapes, rhythm, feel and outcome. We can guide their exploration without needing to instruct on their movement."
>
> Tweeted by Jon Goodwin, 24th May 2018

> "Coach it ugly. If your athlete is nailing every rep then perhaps they're not being challenged enough."
>
> Tweeted by Jon Goodwin, 8th June 2018

As an athlete advances in their mastery of a skill, practice should give the athlete opportunities to explore the skill. In essence, greater knowledge of the skill is promoted by performing the same skill in different contexts. The goal is to encourage the good variability that is seen in skilled performers. Again, constraints can be very helpful in this regard. Once an athlete is proficient in performing a skill in a certain way a new constraint should be introduced that disrupts their performance (in Jon's vernacular – make it ugly). The skill can then be practised until it appears pretty again. Of course, these disruptions can be known in advance or unanticipated, and the practice can be blocked or random...

> "How should we learn and teach? Follow Dr. Seuss: - [2]50 words or less, combined, twisted, and repeated over in a myriad of ways. This is how practice should be."
>
> Tweeted by Steve Magness, 25th July 2018

It is not my intent here to argue that all skills should be learned through guided exploration, not least because some athletes hate it. There is also certainly a role for more traditional modes of instruction. What is probably most important is that skill practice should promote automaticity and good variability in skill performance.

9.6. Learn the competitive skill

When practising skills it is important to practise in a way that will translate to the competitive arena (this is another example of ensuring the transfer of training effects that will be discussed in Chapter 10.6). A good example to illustrate this is to consider a basketball player who is practising shooting. Often when people practise shooting in basketball they take their time in preparing and composing their shot in order to give themselves the maximum likelihood of a successful attempt. However, in a game, time is limited and in most cases a game shot will not appear like a practice shot. Similarly, a "quick release" to your shot can be a deciding factor in determining if you are able to get your shot off. In addition, most game shots are not taken from a standing stationary position where the ball has been in the player's hands for some time – instead they are either taken immediately following receipt of the ball (catch and shoot) or off the dribble. It is thus vital that at least some of the time that a basketball player practises these various different skills. This is not to argue that there is no place for more calm, controlled shooting practice – just that it represents a more general skill.

> "[Agility] who wins? Normally the one who starts first. Practise manipulating space, manoeuvring opponents, standing opponents up, slowing opponents down. Learn to recognise when the constraints are in your favour and then be the first to go."
>
> Tweeted by Jon Goodwin, 7th June 2018

It is also paramount to identify all of the skills that are important in the competitive arena. Some of these are not necessarily obviously apparent. For instance, in team sports one way to ensure that you win a race is to make sure you are the one who says "go". For instance, basketball is a sport which favours the attacking player, as is evidenced by the high scoring nature of the game. When learning to play the sport, a lot of young players spend a long time trying to develop skills of misdirection in order to unbalance their opponent. These can be useful skills, but are often unnecessary given that the contest is weighted towards the attacker. For instance, in many cases it is not necessary to misdirect the defender prior to a jump shot – if you simply shoot without any hesitation you will often have the time to get the shot off. Similarly, fundamental skills like occupying the right space or choosing the correct route to the goal are highly trainable.

9.7. A (first) note on dynamic systems theory

Later in this book (Chapter 15.10) I caution against (rant about?) coaches and athletes trying to be too clever. As I will discuss, a prime example of this in strength and conditioning is the current trend to talk about dynamic systems theory (DST). The content in this chapter around variability and constraints based learning largely encompasses the majority of the useful training insight that can be gained from a consideration of the key aspects of DST. It should be noted however that these conclusions can still be reached without appeal to DST (as illustrated in this chapter). Similarly, there is no need to mystify things by talking about "attractor states" or "self organisation".

10 WHAT TO TRAIN

10.1. Introduction

It is entirely possible that some readers of this book will think its structure is entirely backwards. In particular, so far this book has consisted of a very extended discussion of the organisation of training but there has been no consideration of how an athlete or coach decides what to train. This question will be addressed now. In particular, in this chapter we will see how the integrated analyses of sport, athlete and training activities provide the blueprint for training.

10.2. Needs analysis of the sport

The first part of our analysis is to identify the demands of the sport and from these to work out the types of skills and capacities that an athlete will need in order to be successful in the sport. A common pitfall when people perform this type of analysis is to simply describe the sport and its physiological demands. Such a descriptive account does not on its own tell us the type or level of skill or capacity that an athlete needs to attain to be successful in their sport. So for example, a purely descriptive account of Premier League football might tell us that players cover a distance of 10km within a game or give the proportion of distances that are covered at different speeds. However, this on its own doesn't tell us what level of cardiovascular fitness (for instance, their maximal oxygen uptake) is required to meet these demands.

Similarly, another common mistake when performing a needs analysis of a sport is just to provide a detailed physiological profile or description of the ideal athlete. So in the case of the footballer we provide details about the typical levels of maximal oxygen uptake that are seen at various professional and amateur levels or normative scores on repeated sprint tests. However, this also doesn't provide a strong basis for training decisions as it does not provide a critical evaluation of the factors that are most likely to be decisive in competition. Continuing using the example from above, in football what might be important is not the overall distance that is covered, but rather that the athlete maintains their ability to sprint at top speed in the second half of a match. The athlete's aerobic fitness may be part of the foundation of this ability (i.e. a certain maximal oxygen uptake is a pre-requisite capacity) but the actual determinant of performance might be something else (e.g. some type of measure of their ability to do repeated sprints without a large decrement in speed, their work capacity or their muscular endurance).

Another example of the thought process inherent to a needs analysis can be elucidated by considering injury within the sport. At the most descriptive level the needs analysis will just describe the type and prevalence of injuries in the sport. The next level of analysis will seek to understand why these injuries tend to occur in that sport for instance, by describing the way in which the structures of the body are pathologically loaded when injury occurs – that is the mechanism of injury. The deepest level of analysis will consider the types of skills and capacities that an athlete will need to develop in order to reduce the risk of such injury events occurring or ameliorate the severity of the injury when they do occur.

10.3. Needs analysis of the athlete

Having performed our needs analysis of the sport we are now able to describe the physiological profile of the ideal athlete. This is not simply a list of characteristics, but rather is a critical evaluation of the relative importance of skills and capacities within the sport, how they relate to one another and how they are developed. At this point we now need to analyse the specific athlete we are working with in order to see how their personal skills and capacities compare to the ideal model. Again, this is an evaluative process – we need to identify the most important gaps between the ideal and reality, not simply point out every gap.

The evaluation of the athlete entails multiple considerations. Firstly, we need to understand their current performance capability, and try to understand the factors that may be limiting performance. These factors may be related to, or could be influenced by, deficiencies in the athlete's skills and capacities. At the same time, we need to consider the health of the athlete – what do we need to do to improve the athlete's physical and mental condition, keep the athlete training, reduce their risk of injury, and improve their quality of life.

Once we have performed the needs analysis of sport and athlete we are then in a position to propose a training manifesto (see the next chapter). That is, we can identify training goals for the near, mid and long term future. These goals should be specific and measurable. The next stage is then to identify the type of training that will allow us to reach these goals.

10.4. A note on understanding what is important

The identification of training goals that are consistent with an improvement in overall performance capability is far from simple. Often it will require a deep understanding of the sport, and how skills and capacities are related. I will try to illustrate this with reference to the example of training to improve maximal sprinting speed.

Let's say that the key deficiency that was affecting performance that we identified from our needs analysis was the maximum speed of our athlete. As we saw in Chapter 2, the ability to express high forces in short time periods is a key determinant of maximal sprinting speed. Thus if our needs analysis also suggested our athlete was also weaker than the ideal, then we might conclude that a lack of general strength capability was the root cause of their slow top speed. In this case, improving maximum strength and rate of force development might be the most important training goals, and could result in large, profound improvements in maximal speed.

It is also very important to realise that in many cases, the activity that is most likely to result in performance improvements is practice of the sport itself – and that the majority of training time will rightly be spent practising the sport. However, this is not an argument for the abandonment of other training modalities – far from it. Instead, the role of other types of training may be to ensure that the athlete can spend as long as possible practising their sport (for instance by improving their work capacity) or reducing their likelihood of getting injured. At the same time, although training the sport itself may lead to the largest direct improvements in performance, this also does not justify every training session being focussed on the sport. In fact, the law of diminishing returns justifies an athlete performing supplementary training if they are getting an adequate number of sport specific sessions. For instance, if an athlete already plays basketball 10 times a week, there will probably be more performance benefit to them adding 2 or 3 strength and fitness training sessions than 2 or 3 more basketball sessions.

10.5. Choosing training activities

Once we have a list of training goals we then need to identify the means by which we will achieve them. The first part of this process is in identifying the nature of the training activities that will be most optimal in reaching these goals. The remainder of this chapter will focus on this question. Once training activities have been identified, the details of the training programme can then be established based upon the principles we have discussed at length in the preceding chapters.

10.6. Transfer of training effects

It is generally pretty clear that practising your sport will improve your performance capability within it, both by enhancing your skill level and the relevant capacities that are required to be successful in the sport. A key assumption that underpins most approaches to training is that the performance of certain related tasks can also enhance your sporting performance. For instance, in order to perform effectively over the course of a match, a football player requires a well developed level of endurance. Of course, this could be developed by playing football however the constraints of the game might make it difficult to overload the endurance energy systems most optimally. Thus it is generally accepted that doing general endurance training (e.g. running, cycling, rowing) can aid football performance provided that it is focussed on the energy system demands of football.

The last sentence of the above paragraph exemplifies the most important consideration that we should have when planning a training programme. We need to ensure that if we perform a training activity that is not the sport itself that the adaptations that we hope to gain from the training will enhance our sporting performance. In the above example the consideration was based upon energy systems. Football requires a particular mix of aerobic and anaerobic abilities and we need to make sure that our endurance training is focussed on improving them.

The imperative to ensure that our training is useful to our competitive performance is described as the need to ensure that we have a transfer of training effects. That is, when we train we provide a stimulus to adaptation that results in a training effect. We need to make sure that the training effect is relevant to our competitive goal, and equally that we will be able to incorporate our new capability within our competitive performance. Note that the latter does not necessarily follow even if we improve in a relevant area.

10.7. What is specific training?

The most common way that people try to ensure that they will have a transfer of training effects is to seek training activities that are "specific." However, there is a great deal of misunderstanding as to what specific means and it is common for potentially highly productive training approaches to be sacrificed on the altar of specificity.

A misunderstanding of specificity is particularly common in resistance training for sports performance. It is very common for people to consider specific training to only be activities that look similar to the sport itself. So for instance, if you are a shot putter, specific resistance training might be performing the shot put with a heavier or lighter implement. Such training is considered "specific" because the movement is largely the same as the sporting movement, only the load used is different. Of course, such an activity may be a very valuable training activity. However, this does not mean that other activities that less closely visually resemble the sporting skill itself might not be equally beneficial.

The example described above is an example of people giving primacy to the visual appearance of a sporting skill. This is entirely understandable – it is natural for us to give weight to things that we can see, and harder for us to consider the importance of things that are less visible. In the context of movement however, and as we saw in Chapter 2.2, the most important determinant of performance in a very wide range of activities is our ability to express force. Thus an alternative criterion for determining whether a training activity is specific is to consider how similar the nature of the force expression is to the sporting skills that we want to improve. For instance, at a superficial level, Olympic style weightlifting does not seem to share much in common with vertical jumping. However, Olympic weightlifting is a fantastic tool for training the ability to express force rapidly, and the postures in which peak forces are expressed are very similar to the postures in which force is expressed during vertical jumping. Thus a mechanical analysis of Olympic weightlifting suggests that it is actually a pretty specific training modality for improving vertical jump ability (a contention that is borne out by empirical evidence[20]).

In strength and conditioning, the above considerations are encapsulated in the principle of dynamic correspondence. That is, if we are trying to determine how specific a training activity is to a given skill we analyse the dynamic correspondence between the two movements. This process involves comparing the two movements on a range of criteria that includes, but is not limited to, the visual appearance of the movements and the force that is expressed during them[17,34].

Similar analyses as to what training is specific can also be advanced across the range of training modalities. It is always important though that these are based on the fullest possible understanding of the capacities and skills that are of importance within a given activity. For instance, in the previous section we talked about the endurance capacities that are required in football. One way of evaluating this is to consider the work to rest ratios exhibited by football players and then to structure our training in the same way. This is likely to stress the endurance system in a similar way to a football game. However, this reasoning does not imply that training that uses different work to rest ratios is not specific. Provided that a training modality or a programme of training is designed to improve the endurance abilities required by a football player with an appropriate mix of (say) aerobic and anaerobic abilities, then the training should be considered specific.

Finally, one thing that should always be at the forefront when planning training is that we do need to provoke a training effect. This imperative is something that is sometimes neglected when people design specific training exercises. So for instance, we might design a resistance training exercise that we consider to be specific for sprinting due to its visual similarity and the fact that force is expressed in similar postures. However, if the athlete is not able to express high levels of force in the exercise it is unlikely that they will garner sufficient overload to promote a substantial training adaptation.

10.8. Thresholds

It is important to recognise that the transfer of training effects to the sport is not necessarily linear. For instance, if I improve my squat strength by 10kg this doesn't necessarily mean that my sporting performance will be enhanced. Similarly, if my sporting performance is enhanced by the 10kg improvement in squat strength this doesn't mean that if I improve my squat by another 10kg that I will get an additional improvement in performance that is equal to the first improvement.

Instead, the transfer of training effects often seems to exhibit "threshold" behaviour. That is, an athlete needs to gain a given amount of improvement or reach a certain performance level in the training exercise before they will start to enjoy improvements in performance capability. For instance, if I improve my squat by 10kg this is likely to be largely due to improvements in my squatting skill or capacities that are specific to squatting performance. However, if I improve my squat by 50kg I will be likely to have made profound changes to my overall athletic ability (due to a potential range of different mechanisms). For instance, such a large improvement in strength will probably be in part achieved by the addition of muscle mass – and this mass will be available to me in other tasks. Similarly, because I will have made large changes to my ability to express force with my legs in the squat, it is likely that I will have also improved my ability to express force in a range of other tasks.

An experienced coach will have a sense for the types of training performances across a range of tasks that seem to translate to improved performance capability within the target sport. A deep and thorough needs analysis of a sport will list these types of benchmark, which will in turn help to guide the construction of a training programme.

10.9. General to specific

Within training circles it is common for people to classify training activities on a continuum from general to specific. The basis for this classification will generally be some type of assessment of how closely the activity resembles the sporting activity bearing in mind the considerations described in the previous sections. However, it is important to understand that in this context specific does not necessarily mean better. Instead there is a role for both general and specific training, and the mix of general and specific training modalities will vary based on the characteristics of the athlete and the time of season.

It is generally accepted that a base level of general physical preparation is an important foundation to establish before beginning specific training. For this reason, the training of younger athletes will normally be predominantly focussed on more general training, with more specific training modalities only introduced once the athlete has fully developed the underpinning general qualities. Similarly, the training year is normally structured in such a way that general training activities are performed early in the training year, whereas more specific activities take precedence closer to competition (for those athletes who are mature enough to warrant the use of more specific approaches). Clearly this pattern shares a great deal of common ground with the descriptions of base building, building up and holding back stimuli until they are needed that we have seen in previous chapters.

10.10. Train to be a beast?

"Don't focus on training for your sport. Train to be the baddest mofo, then apply it to your sport."

Tweeted by Christian Thibaudeau, 1st February 2018

Developing specific training approaches can often require an athlete to be innovative and creative. The popularity of these approaches can then be easily understood in terms of the human desire to explore and feel expert (this will be discussed at some length in Chapters 15.9 and 15.10). At the same time, general athletic development – that is, general training that is simply focused on improving a range of the most important general skills and capacities – can often seem less "sexy", and can end up being neglected. This can be a problem for two major reasons. The first is that specific skills and capacities are often developed from a base of generic skills and capacities, and without this base of general training the specific training is less effective. The second is that many athletes have relatively poor levels of general athletic development and only have advanced capabilities in the narrow range of skills and capacities that are directly challenged by their sport. For such athletes, the conclusion of the needs analysis will often be that some general athletic development is the training activity that is most likely to be of benefit to their performance.

The tweet from Christian Thibaudeau which prefaces this section perfectly encapsulates the mechanism by which general athletic development can transfer to sporting performance. In many sports if you improve your speed, jumping ability, body fat percentage, anaerobic fitness etc, you will then be able to apply these new capabilities within the sporting environment. In fact, as a strategy to promote the transfer of training effects, generic training can, paradoxically, be an effective strategy. For instance, a volleyball player who performs non-specific vertical jump training such that they can jump higher in a variety of different training contexts is also likely to jump higher when blocking during a volleyball match.

A further important reason for general athletic development is that such approaches to training tend to be more focused on building and maintaining your "any day level". By this I mean the level of physical performance that you can express on any particular day without any preparatory period or tapering. This is then essentially your stable, base level of fitness – it represents your fundamental characteristics as an athlete. These physical capabilities that you have on a day to day basis are ones that you are practised in using, and that you are likely to be able to bring to bear in the competitive arena. In contrast, specific training approaches will often be more focused on bringing an athlete to a transient peak in performance ability. As these capacities may be to some degree "new", the athlete may not be able to deploy them in competition.

Finally, for many sports the competitive season is long with a large number of competitions. In these sports an athlete's any day level will represent the capabilities that they generally have available to them during competition.

10.11. The special role of strength training

Strength training should probably be a part of almost every athlete's training programme. This probably seems like a bold claim, but its truth can be found if we realise that almost all sports require the expression of force by the athlete. As strength training is focussed on improving the skill and capacity of force expression then the ubiquitous role of strength training becomes apparent.

It's important to emphasize that the above statement does not imply that all athletes should train to improve their maximum strength (it is this type of misinterpretation that often leads people to reject the importance of strength training). Rather, we need to recognise that an athlete will be producing force during performance and that strength training allows them to practise this and also to condition their body to tolerate these expressions of force. It is the latter activity that will quite often be of most benefit to the athlete – loading the tissues to improve their ability to tolerate forces can substantially decrease injury risk.

10.12. The training toolbox

One internet debate that is very common within training circles surrounds the relative merits of this or that training modality. For instance, the use of Olympic style weightlifting exercises in training is passionately advocated by some, whereas others are no less vocal detractors of this training modality. I wanted to close this chapter by addressing these types of debate.

As we have already seen there are a wide variety of ways in which a training stimulus can be applied to our bodies. In this chapter we have discussed how an analysis of the sport, athlete and training activities can be performed in order to pick training activities that are most likely to provide a transfer of training effects to the competitive performance. However, we should recognise that generally there will not be one single optimal strategy – rather there will be a range of approaches that can be followed to achieve the same objective. Another way of describing this is that we have a variety of different tools that we can use in training – there is more than one way to skin a cat. Of course, there may be pros and cons to each approach. However, the root of the internet debates I referred to earlier tends to be the fact that opposing camps fail to acknowledge the pros in other people's approaches, while ignoring the cons in their own.

11 HOW TO TRAIN

11.1. The manifesto

Having performed our needs analysis of sport and athlete we are now in a position where we can set out our training manifesto. Our training manifesto is a statement of the training goals we wish to achieve over the course of the year. In particular, it should provide a broad route map as to how the ultimate goals for the year will be achieved by providing a series of intermediate goals. The manifesto should also be consistent with the long term developmental needs of the athlete – that is, achievement of yearly training goals should represent a logical step along a pathway to fulfilling the athlete's long term needs.

I would suggest 2 particularly important guidelines when formulating a training manifesto. The first is that it should comprise a very limited number of goals – maybe one major goal and at most 2 or 3 supplementary goals. The major goal should be clearly prioritised within the manifesto and subsequent training programme. The second guideline is that in setting goals it is wise to be conservative and realistic. It is important to remember that very profound changes in physical performance capability are achieved by consistent, long term, modest improvements. Seeking faster improvement will threaten adherence to the cardinal rule of training by increasing the risk of injury or overtraining.

11.2. The annual plan

In Chapter 3.7 I introduced the term periodization and promised that I wouldn't mention it much thereafter. When people talk about periodization they are most often talking about the annual training plan – that is the organization of training over the course of one year (although of course we could talk about the periodization of the week or month). Discussion of periodization schemes can be quite technical, and involve terms like linear, block or undulating periodization. However, I believe that annual planning can largely by boiled down to 4 principles that can be used to guide the nature of training across the year:

- The training modes and tasks should be more general during the earlier phases of preparation for a competition and become more specific as the competition nears;
- There should be progressive overload. This tends to be achieved through higher volume in the earlier stages of preparation and higher intensity close to competition;
- The annual plan should comprise the building of a base (and its replenishment) and periods of building up (with or without a peak as appropriate);
- Following the competitive season there should be a period of restorative training, characterised by a wide variety of fun activities, and a focus on recovery.

The different methods of periodization all adhere to these principles, and are largely distinct simply in the way they are applied.

- Linear periodization is the classic model of periodization (see Figure 4.5). There is only one major cycle over the course of the year that starts with high volume, general tasks and moves towards specific tasks performed at high intensity. This type of training is generally used in sports which have only 1 or 2 competitive periods;
- Block periodization consists of short sequenced periods (blocks) of training (accumulation followed by intensification then transformation). The manipulation of volume and intensity and

the choice of general/specific exercises is similar to a linear periodization, but the length of each block is shorter. Block periodization is thus like having 3-6 cycles of a linear periodization within a year;

- Undulating periodization is a different model to the former two as in this case there are not separate periods of high volume and high intensity training. Rather, if you consider a typical training week, the overload on one day might be volume driven, and on another intensity driven.

There is some debate amongst professionals as to the degree that meaningful annual planning is even possible – things can change a lot over the course of a few weeks, and it is pretty difficult to predict how you will react to a given stimulus in 6 months time. It is therefore hard to say with any certainty what your training will look like in 3 months time.

My feeling is that getting the general structure of your training week right is the most important consideration. That is, you need to have a sensible training week that permits lots of light practice sessions such that you are fresh for the hot sessions. You then need to think carefully about how you will build up over the course of a particular cycle (typically 4-6 weeks and certainly not longer than 12 weeks). Trying to plan any further ahead in detail is fraught with difficulty.

The annual plan therefore provides a broad overview of the focus of each training phase or cycle, and shows how these cycles combine to meet the overall goals described in the training manifesto. In terms of annual considerations the 4 principles described earlier in this section suffice for working out exactly what the detail of any particular cycle will look like. Early in the preparation phase is the time to work on more foundational skills and capacities, using more general training modes and tasks, and focus on building a foundation using more volume driven approaches. Closer to competition the choice of training modes and exercises will be more specific and overload will tend to be achieved through increases in intensity with more of a focus on "building up".

11.3. The weekly plan

In Chapter 6 I provided a detailed description of the structure of training. This was largely a description of the weekly structure of training – representing my belief that this is the most important consideration when planning training. The purpose of the annual plan is simply to give a broad overview of the key goals in a given phase of training and the main mechanism by which these will be achieved (e.g. through a volume or intensity overload). Given these broad parameters, it is then possible to plan the training week according to the considerations outlined in Chapter 6.

11.4. The monthly (?) plan

The other key choice that needs to be made for each training phase is the balance between base building and building up, and the particular way in which these will be achieved. These decisions will factor into the planning of the weekly schedule. For instance, if the intention of a phase is to emphasise building up a particular quality through higher intensity activity then it might be particularly important to ensure freshness for the hot sessions. It makes sense for the length of the cycles to be based upon the base building or building up strategy, rather than being arbitrarily determined by the calendar (hence the reason why I have questioned the "monthly" part of the title of this section).

The annual plan will guide the degree to which a given cycle emphasises base building or building up. In general, base building will be an emphasis in the early season, whereas building up will be more prominent later in the season. Chapters 7 and 8 provide guidance on how training variables can be manipulated from week to week across a training phase in order to achieve these ends.

11.5. Example

In Chapter 6.7 I outlined the weekly structure of training for a middle distance runner. This will largely remain the same throughout the season. The major influence of the annual plan on the training schedule will be in dictating the nature of the hot sessions and the volume of practice.

In winter training the athlete will focus on building their aerobic base – they will perform more easy runs during this period and they will tend to be of a longer duration. Hot sessions are focussed on methods that tend to build aerobic capacity. So for instance, the weekend session might be a long run. The Tuesday and Thursday sessions involve longer intervals or threshold running. Some residual tiredness from previous sessions can be tolerated in the hot sessions. During this period the athlete will race in cross country meets – these will tend to be much longer races than will be raced in the summer, and probably represent more threshold training. They generally won't be emphasised – the athlete won't taper their training for them – but they will be raced in order to practise the skills of racing. Winter is also a good time to spend focussed time in the weight room working on strength and tissue conditioning. Finally, the athlete should still practise running fast – often by running relaxed strides.

In contrast, in spring as the athlete builds up to the competitive season their focus will switch to activities that develop their anaerobic metabolism while trying to hold onto their aerobic base. They will still run frequently, although they will drop a few easy runs. The volume of running will also be reduced by shortening the length of all easy runs. Two of the hot sessions will now probably become track sessions – intervals run above, below and at race pace as briefly described in Chapter 8.12. The final hot session might now become a threshold session – this is an activity that should support the maintenance of the aerobic base. The athlete will still visit the weight room, but the length of these sessions will drop considerably. Above all, the athlete must be fresh for the track sessions.

What is important to note in the above two paragraphs is how different the character and emphasis of training can be within a very similar weekly structure. In addition, the plan is very flexible. There are plenty of ways in which the volume and intensity of the programme can be autoregulated based upon the athlete's response to training. Similarly, because the plan is based on a weekly structure and on broad principles, subsequent phases of training are not too dependent on the preceding training. This allows the coach to be responsive with regards to events and incidents that could positively or negatively disrupt the initial planned sketch for the season.

11.6. The session plan

Having gone through the above stages, we will now have a rough idea of all of the different sessions that will be performed during a given training cycle. It is now worth having a brief discussion as to the structure of individual sessions. In particular, most sessions tend to share the following features, although these are by no means hard and fast rules.

- The session will commence with some type of warm up. This is generally designed to prepare an athlete for activity by priming the key systems that will be used. Warm ups will almost always engage the cardiovascular system by including some type of pulse raising activity. Another common warm up activity is to mobilise key structures, in order to ensure that the athlete has the full range of motion available to them that is required for the exercise task. Warm up can also include activation or potentiation activities that are thought to prepare particular muscles or motor patterns for efficient activity. Warm up can also include the rehearsal of key movement skills or mental preparation;
- It is very common for activities that require high degrees of freshness to be placed towards the start of a session, after warm up. These tend to be activities that require the athlete to perform at high intensity, that involve the expression of high rates of force development or velocity, or that are particularly demanding in terms of coordination. These activities will be the focus of the session, and give it its character. In some cases such activities might be performed later in a session – such a decision is taken when the training goal is to perform them under some degree of fatigue;

- After the focus activities have been performed, it is then common to perform activities in an order that reflects their fatigue/freshness requirements. The ordering of the session therefore is based upon the same type of considerations that were described in Chapter 6 for the training week. Of course, there will need to be compromises made here, as the athlete will become progressively more tired as the session continues. Generally, more important exercises will be performed earlier in the session, unless the activity can be productively performed when the athlete is fatigued;
- Activities that are performed towards the end of the session tend to be ones with low freshness requirements. These are activities that the athlete just has to "get done" and that don't necessarily require high levels of focus (for instance, higher volume activities with low intensity, mobility work or stretching, isolated "core" training, etc). This is a good place for base building, even in sessions where the earlier activities are focussed on building up;
- It is also common that sessions are concluded with activities that are designed to aid the recovery process – for instance, low intensity cardiovascular activity that is designed to keep the blood circulating in order to encourage optimal removal of waste products from the blood.

It is interesting to note that the structuring of each individual session is guided by similar considerations as the structure of the week, especially with regards to the management of fitness and fatigue, and the incorporation of base building. As outlined in Chapter 6.8, this is a good example of the fractal structure of training.

11.7. The athlete's life cycle

One aspect of the training process that I have not touched on in much detail in this book is the long term development of athletes. That is, how does the "training" of an 8 year old differ from that of a 16 year old or a 25 year old? This is another good example of the fractal structure of training – the balance of training across the life cycle from childhood to peak performance and beyond, will tend to resemble an annual cycle. In particular, children should perform a wide range of general activities (analogous to the early part of a season) with little or no specific training. Similarly, the emphasis should be on movement quality and learning skills, and on training with the minimum effective dose. As an athlete matures, and becomes more elite, they will begin to specialise in a given sport (this should not happen early) and their training will become more specific. Similarly, with increasing specialisation they will need to use more demanding and potentially novel methods in order to keep improving. Note that it is still likely that the early part of their season will consist of more general training. Finally, training in middle and older age will often more resemble the post competition restorative phase, with an emphasis on activities that promote health and optimal physical function.

12 HOW TO TRAIN FOR...

12.1. Introduction

In this chapter I will discuss specific approaches to training in 6 different sports. These discussions are not intended to be exhaustive, but rather to exemplify the material that has been presented so far in this book - that is, to show how the various concepts that have been discussed actually apply in practice, and how the needs analysis of the sport shapes these choices.

The reader will be aware that I have frequently used weightlifting, powerlifting and middle distance running as examples to illustrate training principles. I thus don't repeat these analyses here, but I would draw the reader's attention to their existence.

12.2. Bodybuilding

Throughout this book I have gone to great lengths to emphasize the fact that there are both tangible and intangible adaptations to training. In this context, bodybuilding is an interesting sport to analyse as success in the sport is determined entirely by an athlete's tangible adaptations – that is the size and symmetry of their musculature. Consequently the training regimes of bodybuilders are focussed on methodologies that promote these tangible adaptations.

The most important characteristic of a typical bodybuilding programme is that training sessions are predominantly GAS focussed. In the context of this book this should make sense as we have tended to characterise tangible adaptations as being more associated with GAS mechanisms of adaptation. Bodybuilding approaches to training are generally predicated on creating a deep alarm phase, in the hope that the consequent adaptation will be large. To this end, volume tends to be high as more work equals more muscle damage, and similarly bodybuilders use strategies that are known to cause more muscle damage (e.g. "forced" repetitions, eccentric training, training to failure, drop sets, etc). This philosophy also explains the well known bodybuilding maxim of "feeling the burn" – again, the athlete wants to train in a way that creates the largest possible amount of physiological stress.

Of course, because bodybuilding training seeks to create deep alarm phases the recovery time from a particular training session can be substantial and their performance capability can be severely depressed. However, because there is no skill that needs to be practised and the only concern is to maximise tangible adaptation in the form of muscle tissue a bodybuilder will be happy to pay this recovery price provided it leads to the most optimal outcome.

This is not to say that bodybuilders will train infrequently. Instead, they will try to train frequently by training different parts of the body separately to one another. This is advantageous for 2 reasons. Firstly, it allows them to perform a greater amount of work for the muscles being trained in a given session as they are only training one part of the body. Secondly, training in this way means that they don't need to wait until they are fully recovered before they train again. Instead, they train different body parts while waiting for the original body part to recover.

Bodybuilders therefore think in terms of their body part splits, dividing their body into different sections. This is very different to most other sports where the whole body is generally involved in the performance of any particular competitive skill. Unfortunately, as described in Chapter 1.6, this approach to resistance training is very influential across sports, despite the fact that it runs contrary to a philosophy of training movement.

Although bodybuilding is entirely focussed on the tangible, smarter bodybuilders do pay attention to some more intangible factors. Most notably there is a role for simply trying to get stronger in bodybuilding by using methods that are not predicated on causing as much damage as possible – for instance, sets of 1 to 3 repetitions using very heavy loads. There are a number of reasons for this. Firstly, this provides a different way to challenge the body. Secondly, a focus on improving the neural abilities associated with strength probably provides a base for increasing muscle mass, in the same way that increased muscle mass provides a base for increased strength. Thirdly, a stronger athlete is able to use heavier loads in their higher repetition training, which will in turn be more stressful.

12.3. The marathon

Most of the examples of building up that can be found in this book relate to an increase in intensity towards the competition. In contrast, for the beginning marathon runner, the focus is on building up the distance that can be covered in one session. In a classic marathon training programme, the athlete will perform a "long run" on a Sunday, and they will try to progressively increase the distance they cover on this run. Similarly, for the more advanced runner, it is common for there to be a focus on increasing the amount of mileage that is covered over the course of a week. Such high mileages are probably required in order for the athlete to develop the requisite running economy to be successful. However in terms of training for middle and long distance running one of the fundamental constraints is that each step that is taken results in an impact loading of the lower limb. This puts a limit on how much mileage can be performed before injury becomes likely and thus even very elite athletes need to build up mileage cautiously in order to ensure that they give their bodies time to develop a tolerance to this loading.

Marathon training is therefore probably more volume driven than most other activities. However, this does not mean that the structure of the training week that was described in Chapter 6 does not apply. Marathon runners still have hot sessions that to some degree mirror the 3 session a week model of middle distance runners. However, they are less concerned with being entirely recovered for the hot sessions – achieving a high weekly mileage is more important. Similarly, sessions will be orientated towards aerobic aspects of fitness but using the more challenging methods of aerobic capacity development – for instance running at lactate threshold. At least one of the three sessions will be a long run.

12.4. Rowing

Olympic and World Championship rowing events are contested exclusively over 2000 metres. At the elite level, depending on boat class they consequently last between 5½ and 8 minutes. From a purely physiological standpoint considering simply the duration of the race, they are thus "middle distance" events that are slightly longer in duration than mile running. This might suggest that the structure of training in terms of volume and intensity would be similar however, in practice, differences between the natures of the sports and how they are competed mean that the character of training is quite different.

In contrast to running, rowing is a seated sport – the weight of the athlete is borne by the boat and impact loading is much lower. The practical result of this is that the volume of actual rowing training that can be performed is much higher. It is thus typical for overload in rowing programmes to be much more heavily weighted towards volume. The same is true of other endurance sports like cycling and swimming where much of the weight of the body is supported and there are not large impact forces. As an aside, the main limitation to volume in rowing is still injury risk, but in this case injuries from the repetitive loading of the back or rib cage. In contrast, in cycling there is less cyclical repetitive loading of such structures and consequently endurance cycling tends to have even higher training volumes than rowing.

Rowing races are also competed quite differently to middle distance running races. In 1500m and mile foot races it is very common for the race to start slowly. One reason for this is that there is a benefit to not leading the field – the person who is in front suffers the most wind resistance, and so racers can save energy by following someone. This is not a factor in rowing where the athletes must stay in their lanes. The second reason is that racing is tactical, and so there is a big advantage in being able to see what your opponents are doing. In running this means having them in front of you. In rowing however, because athletes travel backwards, it is easiest to see your opponents if you are leading the field. For this reason, rowing races tend to start fast as crews compete for the lead over the first 500m.

This difference in race profile quite clearly leads to different physiological demands. One interesting aspect is that in rowing the ability to start quickly is critical. Rowers need to be able to exert a high power output at the start of the race, when the resistance on the oar is high. This is one reason why in rowing there is a greater need to train to improve the ability to express higher forces. The other important reason is also a result of rowing being a seated sport. This means that the body mass of the athlete is supported by the boat – in contrast to distance running they don't need to support their mass. Whereas in running being light is of paramount importance, in rowing athletes can afford to be heavy. This means that they can train to increase muscle mass with the goal of improving their force expression capabilities.

In rowing it is important that athletes maximise their ability to apply force to the oar. This is another reason for the importance of strength training. Another factor that is important is the length of the stroke. If an athlete is able to move the oar through a greater distance, then they will be able to perform more work in each stroke. This is why rowers tend to be tall. However, the length of the stroke is also trainable. Firstly, a rower needs to be flexible in order to compress as much as possible at the front of the stroke. I have always found it a shame that rowers seem to spend a lot of time stretching, but rarely actually improve their flexibility – I think this is an untapped area for performance enhancement. Secondly, rowers need to improve the "functional length" of their stroke – it is worthless having a long stroke if a lack of postural integrity means that you can't apply force throughout the full stroke.

12.5. Sprinting

Elite sprinters will clearly have an exceptionally high ability to express forces during sprinting. Will a key training goal in this population thus be to increase their general strength capabilities? Let's imagine a scenario where we have 2 sprinters who have equal top speeds, but very different leg strength capabilities in the gym. The athlete who is also strong in the gym may well be relying on a similar capability when they are sprinting. However, the weaker athlete is probably able to express high forces during sprinting because of some other skill or capacity. For instance, perhaps they are very bouncy – that is, they are very good at reusing the elastic energy stored in their muscle tendon unit when they strike the ground.

What is important to recognise in the above example is that in both cases the sprinter is able to express very high forces during sprinting itself. The question arises as to whether they will be able to express these high forces during strength training, and if they are not able to, is there a performance benefit to such training? Remember that a key principle of training is overload – in this case will there be overload if the force in the training exercise does not exceed the force in the sporting activity? Somewhat counter-intuitively, during strength training sessions the weaker athlete will be further from expressing forces that are similar to those seen during running than the stronger athlete, as the load that they can handle will be lighter. It might be argued that such an athlete might be faster if they were stronger, but is this the case if their speed is derived from a different capacity? Similarly, will improving the leg strength of the stronger athlete result in further speed gains? It could be argued that because this is a key capacity for the athlete that the answer is yes, or that because they are already strong that further increases would result in minimal gains (and thus the answer is no).

I am largely of the opinion that for most elite and mature sprinters the key goal in the weight room isn't to improve maximum strength capabilities as these athletes will already have high force expression capabilities in postures that are specific to sprinting. However, the weight room is still very important for these athletes – they need to develop a high level of conditioning in order to tolerate these forces. It is quite common that sprinters are actually at high risk of injury because of their ability to express these forces – they are literally able to tear themselves apart due to the high forces they can express but perhaps not tolerate. This then is a good example of understanding what is important in training in a sport. For the sprinter it is imperative to keep them healthy so that they can perform the specific sprint training, plyometrics, etc that will make them fast. However, in order to do this they need to develop a great deal of work capacity, including improving the tissue's tolerance to loading.

One reason sprinters are so strong is that they tend to be very gifted in terms of their nervous system's ability to quickly recruit muscle. Their neuromuscular systems are highly excitable. This leads to some really interesting characteristics. For instance, sprinters often find the Nordic hamstring exercise really challenging. This is not because they don't have the strength, but rather they are very prone to cramping – which I believe is a function of their excitable muscles. Again, this means that practice time needs to be spent in positions where their nervous system is challenged in this way. For instance, activities like B skipping ask the athlete to exert high forces in the hamstring in a position where it is stretched, a common position for hamstring injury.

12.6. Tai Chi

Most people's conception of Tai Chi will be of old people moving slowly in a park. Certainly, the majority of people who practise Tai Chi today only perform the forms for which it is known. However, at its root Tai Chi is an effective martial art, with a remarkably rounded training system. At the same time, the methods by which Tai Chi is trained are quite different to most training approaches, including some of the approaches outlined here, and thus it is worthwhile to sketch out some of the most interesting similarities and differences here.

When watching a person perform a Tai Chi form it is hard to understand the martial context. Firstly, and most obviously, the movements are performed slowly, which seems entirely contrary to the speed and reflexes that are required in a fight. Secondly, many of the postures and movements seen in the Tai Chi forms do not seem to resemble martial skills. The problem with these critiques is that they are based on just one aspect of the Tai Chi training system. In traditional, martial Tai Chi there is also the practice of punching, kicking and throwing techniques, performed at full speed and against an opponent. To imagine that effective martial skill could be developed without this is nonsense.

However, the Tai Chi form is still an absolutely fundamental part of the training system. In Chapter 9 I described how it is impossible to think through ballistic movements, and kicking, punching and throwing are all ballistic. The developers of Tai Chi took an ingenious approach to solving this problem. At their core, the postures exhibited in the form have the same character and structure as the martial skills themselves. The reason for practising the form slowly is to allow the athlete to try and perfect the structures within the form, seeking the strongest positions and shapes, and developing the strength and mobility to achieve them. However, this practice is separated from the dynamic aspect of performing the martial skills themselves. The assumption in Tai Chi is that by spending a long time practising the best postures these will be absorbed into the full pace skill. However, it should be reiterated that in order to do this it is still necessary to practise the skills at full speed.

Another characteristic of training that is peculiar to Tai Chi and other "soft" martial arts is that practitioners train to change some of their natural reflexes. Probably the best example of this is to consider our reflexive response to force – if someone pushes you then you push back. In Tai Chi however athletes learn to "yield" to force, to move with the push, before finding an opportunity to circle their opponent's force back against them.

Much of the philosophy of Tai Chi then seems to be contrary to the ideas that I outlined in Chapter 9. In particular, the retraining of reflexive responses seems particularly counter-intuitive. This contrast however explains some of the key characteristics of skilful Tai Chi fighting. On the one hand, to become effective as a Tai Chi fighter can take much longer than in other traditional martial arts – the training methods are not based simply on practising the martial techniques alone, but also on changing fundamental movement and remodelling reflexes (the latter of which will take a very long time). However, an expert Tai Chi fighter is a formidable foe, both because of the richness of their training base in movement skills, but also because they behave very differently to other fighters.

This is not to say that the entire teaching and learning philosophy is different to the one outlined in Chapter 9 and there are a lot of important commonalities – for instance, the learning of Tai Chi is very much an exploratory process, with a rich variety of training games that are typified by clever constraints designed to encourage the development of the key skills.

The philosophical basis of Tai Chi is in Taoism. The most widely known Taoist concept is that of Yin and Yang, and this theory of mutually dependent opposites is an important influence on Tai Chi training. Yang is fast, hard and impermanent (among other things) whereas Yin is slow, soft and enduring. In the context of this book, Yang can be equated to the hot sessions of a training week, whereas Yin relates to practice. In terms of time (but not demand), the bulk of a Tai Chi practitioner's training will be Yin – practice of the form, conditioning, meditation, low intensity partner work, but they will also drill skills at full speed, punch the heavy bag and spar.

12.7. "Agility"

As in Chapter 9, many of the ideas here I have taken from Jon Goodwin.

The term agility really refers to two separate skills. The first is an athlete's ability to change direction when the task is known. This is largely a function of their movement skill and their ability to express force. The second aspect of agility relates to the athlete's ability to read the competitive environment, make decisions and then execute a change of direction in a non-ideal situation. Training of agility should challenge both aspects.

Essentially, changing direction involves a combination of slowing down and speeding up and there are a very limited number of ways in which these manoeuvres can be performed. There are some stopping and starting skills, various pivots, some cutting skills (the athlete blocks then takes off in a separate direction), swerving and rolling (spinning). Most athletes will have some type of reflexive pattern for most of these skills. In order to train these skills therefore we just need to set up games to allow athletes to practise them. Races are a necessity in this context – this is the most effective way to get athletes to give a proper effort, and also to push them to do things automatically. These skills can be practised in a relatively closed context until the athlete gets proficient. New constraints can then be added to change the nature of the skill, such that the athlete has a new problem to solve which requires them to vary the same skill. Disruption of the skill in this way can be either closed or open. Open constraints might involve the athlete having to respond to changes in the environment, physical disruption of the athlete themselves by a little push (be careful!) or by changing the goal.

Open disruption of these skills also trains the perceptual/decision making aspect of agility. Similarly, games can be created which challenge perceptual skills more keenly. Games can also be created which challenge an athlete to manipulate their opponent, time or space.

It is important to appreciate the requirement for high force expression in change of direction skills. Many athletes will see a large improvement in the change of direction ability if they improve their strength.

13 RECOVERY

13.1. The recovery dilemma

The concept of recovery from training is a familiar one. After a training bout we experience a decrease in our performance capability. The length of time that it takes for us to regain this capability is the recovery period. A recovery modality is an intervention that we employ that is designed to shorten the length of the recovery period.

Generally the use of recovery modalities makes intuitive sense. If our performance capability is diminished it would seem to be a good idea to try and restore it as quickly as possible. Similarly, we know being able to perform more frequent training sessions would be beneficial. However, such a point of view demonstrates an imperfect understanding of the GAS. From a GAS point of view it is the alarm period that is the stimulus to adaptive compensation. The danger arises that if we artificially shorten the alarm phase that we also compromise the adaptation to the training session. For instance, if we perform a hypertrophy training session we might cause considerable cellular damage to our musculoskeletal system. This damage then prompts a cascade of physiological responses, including further disruption of the body's homeostasis, that ultimately result in new muscle tissue being formed (causing the hypertrophy). However, some recovery modalities are predicated on blunting the physiological reaction of the body to exercise induced damage. By blunting the severity of the reaction to exercise the body can recover quicker, but the stimulus for adaptation is attenuated.

There is also a further wrinkle to the consideration of recovery modalities. It is likely that some recovery modalities are more effective if applied sparingly, and thus we want to preserve their use for when they are most needed.

It is clear therefore that the decision to employ recovery methodologies is much more complex than might be expected. In fact, for recovery it is also important to properly understand the nature of a particular training session, and the expected mechanism of adaptation. For sessions which seek a predominantly GAS mediated adaptive response it will often not be appropriate to employ recovery methodologies that blunt the alarm response. For more practice orientated sessions, the employment of recovery modalities might be less likely to affect the adaptive process, however given that such sessions will tend to be less disruptive to the body's performance capability anyway, the use of artificial recovery modalities could be questioned.

To my mind, most recovery strategies aside from healthy habits like regular sleep and a healthy diet should normally be reserved for competition periods. Competition is likely to be stressful and result in significant alarm periods. However, in this case the alarm period and the consequent adaptation are not necessarily desired. Similarly, the time available to recover between competitions or matches might be short. It seems prudent then to save recovery modalities for the periods when they can have the biggest potential impact on performance (i.e. during competition) rather than employing them in training where in the worst case they may actually compromise the training process.

13.2. Cumulative stress

So far we have characterised the GAS response to training as being the body's adaptive response to a training stress. We have also talked about the specificity of the training stress in promoting the desired adaptations

(Chapters 10.6 and 10.7). However, what we have not considered is the effect of other, non-training related stresses on the adaptive response.

The GAS response is mediated by both global and local mechanisms. At a global level the most significant response to a stressor is the engagement of the fight or flight mechanism which primes the body for action in order to boost the chances of survival in the presence of a threat. The fight or flight mechanism involves the release of a cascade of hormones that circulate in the blood stream and that can thus affect the whole organism. From a training perspective, the local effects of this global response will depend on the nature of the training stress, that is, the structures that are involved in training will be more sensitised to the circulating stress hormones, as well as engaging their own adaptive responses.

What is important to note from the above description is that the global response to stress is to a large part non-specific. For instance, in the presence of a stressor the body will release adrenaline. The nature of the response will be similar if the stressor is a training session, an impending work deadline or the local proximity of a sabre toothed tiger (of course the magnitude of the response might differ). At a global level the body's ability to distinguish between different types of stress is limited.

What this means is that any stress that an athlete is subjected to will tend to create a GAS response that the athlete needs to adapt to, and recover from. Consequently, the effective training load that an athlete is experiencing cannot be based simply on a consideration of the training that they are performing. Instead, if the athlete is subject to significant stresses outside of training these should also be factored into the training load. Put another way, a stressed athlete will not have the same capacity for training and/or they will find it harder to recover from training.

The sum total of the above analysis is that if you want to optimise your adaptation to training then you need to minimise other sources of stress. Of course, this is easier said than done – most of the sources of stress in our lives are either necessary evils (e.g. work) or arrangements that we choose because they enrich our lives (e.g. relationships, children). However, for some athletes the importance of their training goals will mean that they make sacrifices in these areas in order to minimise the cumulative stresses that they experience. For the rest of us, it is simply important to be aware of the impact of all stresses and to adjust our expectations and training programmes accordingly, especially in times of high stress.

13.3. Sleep and routine

Although it may seem like a self-evident truism, it is important to note that rest is by far the most essential recovery strategy and to recognise that sleep is the body's principal strategy for resting. For this reason, if you want to maximise your training gains then the most influential area to look at is your sleep habits. From a recovery perspective this is not just about getting enough sleep in terms of the time spent sleeping – it is also important that your sleep schedule should be regular – that is that you largely go to bed and get up at similar times each day.

The latter guideline may seem counter-intuitive. If you are getting enough sleep why does it matter when you take it? The answer to this question can be found by considering the effect of making a change to our sleep schedule. It is well established that our bodies have diurnal rhythms. For instance, there are daily fluctuations in our circulating hormone levels. One example is the increase in melatonin towards the end of the day that prepares us for sleep. If we break from our normal schedule this represents a large interruption in our body's homeostasis. This is an important stressor, and as we have just seen, will contribute to the cumulative stress that the body is attempting to adapt to. At a more simple level, an irregular sleep pattern implies that there will be times when we have some sleep debt – it is well known that sleep deprivation has negative consequences for performance.

Quantifying the relative effect of an irregular sleep pattern on the training process is, of course, beset by methodological difficulties[30]. However, the impact of a regular and sufficient sleep schedule on the adaption to training is profound and I would suggest that regular sleep is probably much more important than most people consider it to be. Interestingly, a regular sleep schedule with an early bedtime will often be a sacrifice that people are unwilling to make. This reflects not just the self discipline that is required to implement such a schedule but also the level of impediment that such a routine can be to a normal social life. Maximising recovery through sleep is therefore a good example of a recovery strategy that normally only the most dedicated athletes manage to achieve.

13.4. Nutrition

Many (many) books have been written on nutrition, and it is not my intention to reinvent the wheel here. I thus only want to offer a few observations. First and foremost, from a recovery perspective, sleep and diet are the two most important things to get right. However, with nutrition it is very easy to fall into the trap of searching for the magic cocktail of supplements that will support your training. Instead it is much more important to ensure that you are eating a healthy diet with the correct balance of proteins, fats and carbohydrates and with plenty of fresh fruit and vegetables. Your supplement regimen is simply the icing on the cake, and probably not something to focus on until you have got your overall diet right. A focus on supplements is another example of the phenomenon described in Chapter 15 – humans like to innovate and to seek "sexy" solutions to problems. The idea that a healthy diet with lots of vegetables is the most important aspect of nutrition for maximising training improvements simply isn't "sciencey" enough.

Another area that is important is the timing and number of meals. Again, ensuring that you fuel appropriately before and after training and that other meals are taken at the right times is much more influential than is normally considered.

Without meaning to undermine the previous two paragraphs, there are almost certainly dietary supplements that can be helpful to the training process. However, it is hard to ascertain which are effective. The scientific literature is not desperately helpful in this regard – there are only a few supplements that have been supported by research.

13.5. Self management

One recovery activity that I do think can be used productively without worrying too much about blunting the adaptive response is the maintenance of mobility. In the short term, most things that we do in life and training, including not doing anything, tend to decrease the mobility of our joints and the pliability of our connective tissue. If we want to train frequently it is often really worthwhile to spend time restoring these qualities on a regular basis. Such a strategy is consistent with the idea that if we are doing lots of exercise then we should generally feel good. Similarly, the maintenance of mobility means that we are most likely to be able to get the most out of each training session.

13.6. Other recovery strategies

A vast number of different recovery protocols have been described within the training literature. As is the case for supplements, some of these are probably effective however, for many there is a lack of strong scientific evidence supporting their use. It is always worth remembering though that one benefit of a recovery strategy is in simply helping an athlete to feel good – the placebo effect is a well established and powerful phenomenon[11]. Thus to some degree, if a recovery modality provides this, it may well be worthwhile. Above all however, it is important to bear in mind the caveats given around recovery strategies at the start of this chapter – that is, be wary of using a recovery strategy that blunts the adaptive response if it is not necessary.

14 INTENSITY REVISITED

14.1. What is intensity?

Throughout this book we have made constant references to the "intensity" of training, and in Chapter 3.4 I made an attempt to define intensity that was based on the level of performance being exhibited relative to the maximum performance capability of the athlete. Such a definition of intensity is fine as a description of a key variable that can be used to characterise the nature of a training programme. However when taking a wider perspective, there are at least 4 different ways that intensity could be defined that have meaning in the training context:

- Percentage of maximum performance capability: this is the working definition of intensity that has been used so far in this book. However, even this definition has further subtleties. In particular, what "maximum" should be used to express the limit of an athlete's performance capability? Should it be based upon a recent competitive performance or should it take account of daily fluctuations in an athlete's capability (for instance due to fatigue)? Similarly, how do we account for increases in an athlete's performance capability across a training period?
- Level of effort: a different way of defining how "hard" a person is working is simply to ask them. By far the most common way in

which this is achieved is the use of some variation of the "Borg Scale of Perceived Exertion"[9] which asks the athlete to put a number to the effort they have exerted in the exercise. There is a strong relationship between an individual's rating of perceived exertion and more objective measures of the percentage of maximum performance capability. However, an assessment of level of effort also takes into account variations in the daily capabilities of the athlete. In addition, and independent of daily fluctuations, some days a given performance feels easier in some way and thus requires less effort. Similarly, on some days a person has to "work harder" to achieve the same percentage performance level even if their maximum capability is similar;

- Arousal: this is the emotional involvement/investment of an athlete in a performance. We will look at this in depth in the next section;
- Intent: this could alternately be named the focus of the athlete on the performance. This will be covered after the discussion of arousal.

These different "facets" of intensity lead to a number of very important insights with regards to the training process. Overall these can be summarised by observing that getting training intensity right is of critical importance.

14.2. Arousal

When we talk about arousal in the sporting context this is distinct to the common usage of the word arousal to denote an increase in sexual interest/desire. Instead, arousal refers to the level of excitement, stimulation, aggression and emotional involvement experienced by an athlete prior to a performance. For instance, when an athlete "psyches up" for a given performance feat, they are trying to increase their level of arousal. There is a complex relationship between arousal and performance that is often referred to as an "inverted U" relationship[18] (Figure 14.2). That is, there is an optimal level of arousal for performance, and being above or below this level can be detrimental to the performance outcome.

The optimal level of arousal will be highly context specific. For example, in a sport like darts high arousal would be disadvantageous – you would be over-stimulated when the performance of fine motor skills generally requires calm. Conversely, a sport like powerlifting requires a very high level of arousal in order to fully maximise strength performance. It should also be noted that the optimal arousal level can also be specific to the individual, and so the inverted U model is simply a useful starting point.

Figure 14.2. Inverted U relationship between arousal and performance.

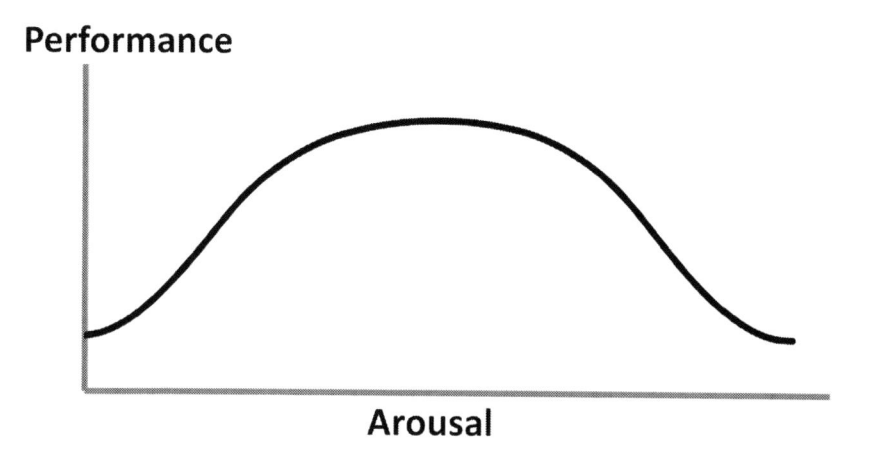

Performance

Arousal

The importance of finding the optimal level of arousal for training should not be under-estimated. It is common for people to make the mistake of assuming that the optimal level of arousal for peak performance is also the optimal level to be achieved in training. In certain contexts, this type of mistake can actually be highly damaging to the training process.

In order to understand the impact of arousal it is worth briefly considering the physiological effects created by increasing arousal. In particular, increasing arousal is a way of activating the body's fight or flight mechanism, by prompting the hormonal system to release adrenaline. The purpose of the fight or flight mechanism is to increase the performance capability of the body in response to a threat – it is therefore very clear to see how this can be engaged to improve a given physical performance. The increase in performance associated with arousal can be very profound.

14 INTENSITY REVISITED

So far, so good, and it does seem like arousal would be a positive thing to encourage during both performance and training. However, such a conclusion neglects consideration of the longer term effects of engaging the fight or flight mechanism. In particular it is important to recognise that high levels of arousal are also highly fatiguing – most of us will have experienced the tiredness that follows a bout of adrenaline inducing activity. This is because the fight or flight mechanism is inherently associated with the GAS. A fight or flight response is an acute response to a very significant stressor, and the consequent alarm phase can be protracted, especially in training where there might also be a significant training stress applied.

Our brief study of arousal thus leads to the following general conclusions. Firstly, that increasing arousal can be a very powerful way of boosting performance in competition or training. Secondly, that such a boost is highly demanding in the short to medium term.

The problem with using increased levels of arousal to boost training performances is that the more pronounced alarm phase will be harder, and take longer, to recover from. In terms of the GAS, this can only be justified if the subsequent adaptation will be greater, and more than compensate for the less frequent bouts of training. Unfortunately, in very many instances this will not be the case. Trying to train with high levels of arousal will often quickly lead to a plateau in an athlete's performance improvements and maybe even overtraining. Higher levels of arousal should therefore largely be avoided in training (or used very sparingly) and reserved for competition.

"Don't eat chalk."

Dan John

In addition, it is also quite challenging to train with higher levels of arousal on a week by week basis. Constant stimulation of the fight or flight mechanism is tiring and it can become harder and harder to get "up" for the performance. One little acknowledged advantage that is gained by athletes who abuse steroids is the so called "roid rage". The drugs not only aid recovery of physical structures like muscle tissue, but also allow the athlete to engage the fight or flight system more regularly — they are able to bring emotional investment and aggression to many more training sessions.

14.3. Intent

"All movements are motivated by Yi (mind/intent) not external form."

Chang San-Feng, Tai Chi Chuan Ching

The above quote is generally attributed to Chang San-Feng the mythical founder of Tai Chi. It describes how movement is directed by "Yi". The appropriate translation of Yi into English is challenging with many commentators settling on some combination of mind and intent. The same challenge arises when trying to define the meaning of intent in terms of the training context. Earlier in this chapter I characterised intent as being akin to focus. This is true, but is only half the picture. In particular, what are we focussing on?

The nature of intent will tend to be task specific. Generally it will encompass technical and performance considerations. From a technical point of view we will try to perform the movement as accurately as possible (subject to certain caveats). The performance focus will generally be focussed on the expression of the key quality inherent to the task. For instance:

- In weightlifting and powerlifting our intent is to move the bar as quickly as possible, even if the load is large and thus the actual speed of the bar is slow. In doing so we maximise our rate of force development, and encourage adaptations that improve our capacity to accumulate a large amount of impulse in a small amount of time;
- In sprinting our intent is on relaxation at high speed. Similarly, in longer distance running we seek relaxation and economy of movement, particularly as we fatigue;
- In martial arts our intent is on effectively delivering force through our target by transferring force from the ground, through our hips to our foot or hand.

14 INTENSITY REVISITED

To summarise, when we train we should not just be going through the motions. Rather, we are mindful of the way in which we are moving, and we try to perfect our technique such that the external and internal manifestations are as effective as possible.

14.4. What is the right attitude?

So far in this chapter we have seen that higher levels of arousal can help improve training performances but that they have a prohibitively high price in terms of recovery time. Instead I have argued that we should have "intent" when we train – that we strive to move perfectively with high levels of effectiveness. I am sure that for many readers such a strategy will also sound exhausting. How can we train with intent without feeling a constant psychological pressure to be perfect or having the cognitive drain of constantly monitoring our movements?

"Mindfulness means moment-to-moment, non-judgmental awareness."

Jon Kabat-Zinn

The answer to this question lies in mindfulness, and in particular being non-judgmental. When we train we should be constantly aware of how we are moving. We move with intent and focus on executing our movements to the best of our current abilities. However we don't attach value to the degree to which we meet the ideal of perfection – we are simply aware of how we are doing and use this information to guide our next actions. In essence, we strive for perfection, but it doesn't matter to us if we don't attain it.

Such an attitude towards training can, of course, take time to develop. Many of us are our own harshest critics and thus such an attitude can be quite uncomfortable at first. However, developing an attitude of mindful, non-judgment does not mean that we don't care about the training process. Rather, we demonstrate this commitment in the consistency of our training. During training itself however, we to a large part detach ourselves emotionally from the outcomes of training, both in terms of arousal and technical execution.

It is also important to realise that our goal is not to rigidly control what we are doing with our mind – such an approach would destroy the fluency of our movement. Instead, by being mindful of what is taking place we are able to adjust our movement positively moment to moment.

Finally, being non-judgmental also means that if you need to, sometimes it is OK to just train, without engaging cognitively with the task in question. That is, you just "get it done" without worrying about the quality or focus. This conclusion does come with two caveats though. Firstly, if you are good at training mindfully it should not normally be too demanding to train mindfully. Secondly, if you really don't have the energy to train mindfully, it might be worth considering whether you actually need a break.

14.5. Peaks and plateaus

In Chapter 8.8 I discussed the problem with "peaking" strategies. In brief, the problem is that, by definition, the achievement of a peak means that it will be followed by a large and potentially sustained drop in performance capability. In Chapter 8, I described the realisation of a peak as being the consequence of a planned increase in intensity over the course of several weeks (wave loading) with the peak achieved when the adaptive capacity of the athlete is exhausted.

It is important to realise that if we exhaust our adaptive capacity then we can expect no further improvements from training until we have allowed the adaptive capacity to recover. In the case of wave loading described above, we try to optimise the use of our adaptive capacity in order to promote the greatest training improvements. However, we can also use up our adaptive capacity in sub-optimal ways.

Probably the biggest drain on adaptive capacity is performing an activity at the limit of our performance capability. This should make good intuitive sense – if we perform an activity maximally this creates a very large training stress, and a large amount of adaptive capacity is depleted in the recovery and adaptation process. For many athletes and activities it requires only a very limited number of maximal performances to completely exhaust the adaptive capacity. This then leads to the conclusion that performing maximally will often very quickly cause performance capability to either peak or plateau.

Training at maximal or near maximal intensity is therefore a training strategy that needs to be used judiciously and sparingly due to the risk of inducing a plateau in training improvements. It is similarly important to realise that training with maximal intensity with high levels of arousal increases the likelihood of exhausting an athlete's adaptive capacity. This is one of the reasons why it is generally wise to restrict most maximal efforts to the competitive arena (Chapter 16.3). The major caveat to this is of course if the athlete needs to practise the skill of performing a maximal effort because that is their competitive sport. However, in this case there are strategies that can be employed to ameliorate the effects of this practice on their training status.

Interestingly, the ability of an athlete to tolerate maximal intensity training is to a large part dependent on the size of their base. An athlete with an inadequate level of base training will quickly stagnate if performing higher intensity training, whereas the ability to train at higher intensities can be improved by expanding the tank. The ability to perform repeated bouts of near maximal activity can be important in the competitive environment. For instance, in major track and field athletics championships the athletes generally have to compete in multiple races across the course of several days if they are to reach the final. If considering the example of a 1500m runner, they will often need to compete in 3 races separated by only a day's recovery. This requires a much more extensive aerobic base than is required if simply competing in a one-off race.

The above discussion provides a good illustration of why athletes should be cautious when training at higher intensity. Higher intensity training will tend to induce a greater alarm phase, which will be harder to recover from. At the same time, this will provide a powerful stimulus for training adaptations. Generally therefore, it is prudent to reserve phases of higher intensity training for when they are really needed. Similarly, higher intensity training will also quickly deplete the tank and the athlete should be mindful of this.

14.6. Try not to grind

Throughout this book I have been at pains to emphasise the practice considerations inherent to training. This also ties in well with a cautious approach to maximal intensity training. When we perform an activity at near maximal intensity it is likely that our execution will not be technically perfect. We want to limit the amount of non-perfect practice in our training.

In resistance training, maximal intensity training is often typified by lifts that are a "grind". That is the lift is a real trial of attrition, that is slow, and where the athlete will do whatever is required to move the bar – including sacrificing technique. There are all sorts of strategies that can be employed in order to try and encourage an athlete to avoid the grind. For instance, velocity based training is based on the fact that generally, as the load used within an exercise is increased, the velocity of skill execution is reduced. By prescribing a desired velocity for the exercise it is possible to ensure that an athlete lifts at an appropriate intensity. Similarly, an athlete can be given the goal of performing a given amount of repetitions within a certain time period. If the training is adequately "dense" then the athlete will be limited in the load that they can use.

An alternative approach is to perform maximal or near maximal efforts when fatigued. The advantage of this is that an athlete can practise limit efforts, but without expressing their "true" maximum. Similarly, this approach is less challenging to an athlete's ego – they are more likely to fight to retain good technique, rather than prioritising successful completion of the lift above all else.

14.7. Knowing when to stop (and rest)

"400 meter repeats; twenty of them in total with a scant 60 to 90 seconds of rest in between. Starting at 60 seconds per 400 meters, and ending number 20 in a blistering 50.1 seconds. This mind-blowing workout comes from the log of Alan Webb, performed in the weeks leading up to his American

Record (3:46) in the mile. ... What struck me wasn't the awe-inspiring workout, but what he did the following day; he rested, completely."

"One of the lessons that I've learned in coaching elite runners is that when you are riding the razor's edge of stress and recovery, when you have a phenomenal day, that isn't a signal to push forward, it's a signal to pull back."

Steve Magness, 22/02/18, www.peakperformancebook.net

Hopefully the wisdom in Steve Magness' above quote should seem consistent with the prior messages in this chapter. Most athletes struggle to stop – the insecurity that one hasn't done enough is common. However, after the realisation of a new personal best or an expression of a truly maximum level of performance capability it is certainly a time for pulling back. Pushing forwards is likely to quickly exhaust adaptive capacity and lead to a plateau.

14.8. Your 100% is not the same as my 100%

A novice's maximum performance capability is not the same as an expert's! Of course, this is easy to explain in terms of the expert's development in skills and capacities. However, what is important to realise is that an important part of the expert's higher level of performance is that they are able to use more of their latent capacity than the novice. This can be understood by thinking of the apocryphal story of the old lady who when under stress is able to lift a car to free her trapped grandchild. Our bodies have a greater performance capability than we are able to access voluntarily – let's call this the "true" maximal capability. An important effect of training is to make more of this potential capability available to us.

For instance, one feature of the neuromuscular system is the existence of Golgi tendon organs. As the name suggests, these are mechanoreceptors that are embedded within the tendons. Their function is to sense the tension within the tendon, and if it rises too high to cause the muscle to relax. This is a protective mechanism - it is designed to prevent you from tearing the muscle-tendon unit. However, their existence means that our ability to voluntarily express force with a given muscle is lower than the actual potential maximum capacity of the muscle. One adaptation to strength training is that the Golgi tendon organs are trained to be more tolerant to higher levels of tension. This means that we can get closer to the maximum capacity of the muscle-tendon unit before the Golgi tendon organ forces the muscle to relax.

There are all sorts of adaptations like the one described above that occur with training. The upshot of this is that when an expert exerts a maximal effort their mind and body is much more engaged in delivering the performance and that they are closer to their true maximal capability. This in turn means that an expert's maximal effort is more intense than a novice's.

Figure 14.8. Average training intensity of elite Russian weightlifters compared across competitive levels (higher competitive ability indicated by lighter shade). Figure adapted from Medvedyev[27].

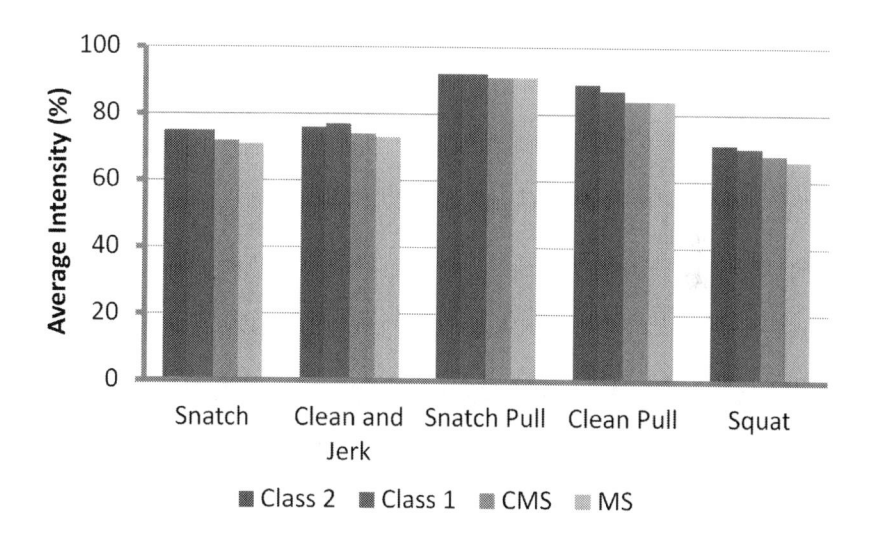

Figure 14.8 displays the average intensities of training of Russian weightlifters in the key competitive and training exercises. What is interesting is that the better weightlifters consistently train at a lighter intensity than their less advanced counterparts. At first glance this probably seems counter-intuitive, and contrary to the principle of progressive overload (at least in terms of progressive overload in intensity). However, it

can be understood in the context of the above discussion – e.g. 70% of maximum is more intense for a more qualified weightlifter. If it was possible to express these intensities relative to the true maximal capability we might find that the intensity of lifting of the more qualified athletes is the same or even higher than the less strong lifters.

15 PSYCHOLOGY AND OTHER PEOPLE

15.1. Introduction

In the previous chapter we revisited the meaning of intensity. Much of the early part of this discussion was centred on arousal and intent – topics that would traditionally be considered to be within the domain of sport psychologists. In this chapter we will touch on a few more aspects of the psychology of training, and also consider the impact of other people on an athlete's training process.

15.2. Patience

The training process is not a sprint. Many of the adaptive processes that are a result of training occur when we are not training (i.e. during rest and recovery periods). Similarly, there are a limited number of (legal) things that we can do to speed up these adaptive processes. Consequently, effective training requires patience and realistic expectations as to the amount of improvement that can be gained in a given period of time.

There is an optimal rate of improvement and trying to improve more quickly than this will generally be counterproductive. To increase the pace of improvement an athlete will need to increase the volume or intensity of training or the rate of progressive overload. These types of decisions can lead to negative consequences. For instance, overtraining is a real risk if the volume and intensity of training is too high. An overtrained athlete will experience a decrement in performance capability and may need to stop training for a period of time. Similarly, injury risk can increase concurrently with increases in the volume and intensity of training.

There are even potential problems in the case where an athlete manages to execute a programme that rapidly takes them to a higher level of performance without negative short term consequences. Such an improvement is likely to represent the realisation of a peak. We have discussed the problems with peaks previously. In particular, there is often a significant period of underperformance after a peak. An athlete whose training profile represents a series of high peaks and low troughs is ultimately unlikely to progress as fast as an athlete who progresses more consistently.

Some simple arithmetic can very powerfully illustrate the potential of small consistent gains. For instance, most people would be ecstatic if they improved their bench press performance by 15kg over the course of a year – such an improvement "only" requires a 1.25kg improvement each month. If this type of improvement could be sustained for 5 years it would take most people to an elite level of performance. Clearly these types of improvement are not normally realised – a fact that serves simply to emphasise that very modest but consistent improvements can lead to immense performance capabilities. Most people's training progressions are not this consistent however, and their capability swings backwards and forwards over the course of a year – and in the worst cases doesn't improve.

The other key role for patience is in making sure that we don't violate the cardinal rule of training. As we know, we are seeking consistency in our training. If we get impatient about a perceived lack of progression this could compel us to abandon our current strategy (or training altogether). This has two disadvantages: firstly, we are inconsistent in our training, violating the cardinal rule; and secondly, we don't learn whether the training programme we were following was effective or not. Instead it is of paramount importance that we trust the training process and that we don't spend time dwelling on the amount or pace of our progression. Training outcomes should be judged in the same way as investments – in the long term.

15.3. The myth of "giving 100 (and 10) %" and the actual challenge

The persuasive myth of the importance of giving 100% pervades our society and is particular prevalent in sport. I hope that the falsehood inherent in such an approach (certainly if applied to training) should be readily apparent to the reader who has reached this point in this book. Such a contention can be challenged on a number of levels:

- We have seen that well structured training programmes consist of a relatively high volume of light activity, punctuated by bouts of more intense training. I have explicitly argued that training too hard in light sessions is counter-productive. That is, we should be mindfully not training at 100% most of the time;
- We have seen that the kind of emotional arousal that is required to give 110% is largely detrimental to the training process;
- We have seen that even the instruction to emphasize intent has its caveats.

A misguided attempt to give 100% to training (in the traditional understanding) will not be the most effective approach. This is a hard message for many people to internalise, particularly athletes who will often pride themselves on their exemplary work ethic.

What then is the actual challenge involved in following a successful training programme? Again, this is something where we rely on the cardinal rule of training – the challenge is to remain consistent. It should be noted that this is probably no easier than "giving 100%" – it is just that the nature of the challenge is different. Improving your performance capability is not about completing arduous workouts punctuated by periods of rest. Instead it involves a commitment to consistent training. It means putting in the practice, day in and day out. The challenge lies in getting out and performing a light, routine training session even on the days when you really, really don't feel like it.

The other major challenge also emerges from the cardinal rule of training – in this case the corollary to not do things that will prejudice your consistency. This challenge is far reaching and can require great feats of discipline. At the elite level it can be as extreme as sacrificing work or social goals in favour of training. It also entails the discipline to stick to the training plan, through both good and bad periods (the former often being harder as the temptation to attempt more when you are feeling good is very hard to resist).

It is interesting to note that the myth of 100% is actually contrary to the cardinal rule of training. An athlete who always trains with this intensity is more likely to experience injuries or periods of overtraining. In addition, the day to day to challenge of getting out and performing some type of training is harder if you are constantly tired.

15.4. The power of expectation and the importance of environment

> "They can, because they think they can."
>
> Virgil, The Aeneid

In Chapter 2.9 I talked briefly about nature versus nurture with a focus on stressing that our ability to change our physical performance capabilities is actually relatively large – and probably much larger than most people think. Understanding and internalising this idea is a very important aspect of a successful training programme. In particular, our expectation as to the types of performance we are ultimately capable of will tend to be a self-fulfilling prophecy – hence the Virgil quote above.

For this reason it is important to surround yourself with people who are good at the thing that you are training in. They then act as models of the levels of attainment that are possible. The best models are those who have come from a similar place as you have, or that you feel you should be able to compete with. The achievements of these types of people are then powerful examples in raising your own expectations of what is personally possible.

Expectation is just one example of how environment can be a decisive factor in the success of a training programme. As we have just seen in the previous section, one of the key challenges in training is maintaining your consistency. This is another area where environment can be pivotal in facilitating the training process. It is much easier to stay motivated and to maintain your consistency if you are one member of a group who support each other in staying on track.

I think that most people would consider the main benefit of a positive training environment to be the atmosphere that can be generated by a bunch of like-minded people training hard together and supporting one another. There is no doubt that such an atmosphere can be highly facilitative of great training performances, and this certainly plays a role in the effectiveness of having a good training environment. However, as we have seen, the achievement of impressive training performances is only one small part of a training programme. It is my belief that the effects of environment on expectation and consistency are the more profound benefits.

15.5. Caring too much and the need for a coach

Many athletes are deeply invested in the training process – sporting competition is a big part of their life and they spend many hours training to improve their performance. At the same time, it is common for athletes to also spend a lot of time thinking about training and competition – exactly because it is a big part of their lives, and represents one of their major interests. In some cases however, such a large emotional and intellectual connection to the training process can be a negative factor in the training process.

15 PSYCHOLOGY AND OTHER PEOPLE

Some athletes will have a tendency to spend considerable time ruminating about training, worrying about training outcomes or questioning the choices they have made in planning their programme. This can lead to a number of negative consequences. First and foremost, if an athlete is constantly worrying about their training then this is a potential source of stress. In Chapter 13.2 we saw that the body has a limited capacity to distinguish between different types of stress. We thus want to avoid unnecessary stress that does not serve to promote desired adaptations, and worry about the effectiveness of a given training process certainly falls into this category. The other potential problem with constantly evaluating your training choices is that it is a behaviour that can lead you to violate the cardinal rule of training. That is, athletes who are constantly questioning what they are doing, or thinking about other approaches are much more likely to frequently switch between programmes, leading to an inconsistent training approach.

The ideal attitude of an athlete towards training is somewhat different to the stereotype. Of course, a deep commitment to the training process is a prerequisite for success, as is the discipline to stick to a consistent training plan. However, on a day to day basis it is much more productive for an athlete to not really think about training outside of training sessions. (A potential exception to this might be visualisation of competitive performances etc, however I would contend that these activities themselves are training and should be ring-fenced from everyday life by being performed in timetabled, dedicated sessions). This then allows the athlete to recover more optimally. Of course, this laissez faire attitude normally only exists outside of the training sessions.

One little acknowledged reason why coaches are so valuable is that they make such an approach much easier to achieve. The key requirement here is that the athlete has trust in their coach. If this exists, the athlete can mentally delegate all responsibility for evaluating the effectiveness of training to the coach. This division of roles is highly advantageous – the athlete simply focuses on training consistently with the appropriate degree of intensity, and making sure that they recover optimally. The coach's job is to worry about the effectiveness of the training programme and whether the athlete will be in peak shape for the most important competitions.

15.6. Getting help

Do get help!

In the previous two sections we have explored some of the ways in which training partners and coaches facilitate the training process. Most fundamentally, it is remarkably difficult to be consistent in your training (in all senses of the word) if you attempt to go it alone. Training partners and coaches can make this task much easier.

It is also a good idea to involve other people in your training process as they can offer a more objective assessment of your strengths and weaknesses. Such input is important even for highly knowledgeable experts in training – we all tend to have a blind spot when it comes to ourselves. Similarly, one reason why it is often better to have a coach who you trust write your programme is that they will be more likely to challenge you in uncomfortable but positive ways. Most of us if left to our own devices will tend to perform the type of training that we enjoy doing, and may skimp on training that we dislike but need.

15.7. Resolutions, starting and failing

Grand resolutions don't work. The main reason for this is that they tend to be posed in terms of absolutes – e.g. from the 1st January I will train every day. The problem with absolutes is that they are not very forgiving of failure. For instance, if on the 4th January I don't train, where does that leave me? The resolution is now "broken" and is thus not in force anymore. I thus don't train on the 5th or 6th January. I then have a word with myself, remind myself of my goals, and resolve to start training every day again. However, today is Thursday and it is neater to start a new plan on a Monday and so I postpone the new regime until then...

I believe that it is desirable to avoid making resolutions. Instead, if you want to change something or start doing something, just start. The earlier you can start the better – don't put off starting until a better time. Your attitude to the new activity should be that you are trying to instil a new habit. You will have some idea what you want that new habit to ultimately look like. For instance, maybe it is that you will train every day. Once you have made the decision to work towards a new habit your goal is simply to do the best job you can of behaving in that way. Over time as you increase the frequency of the habit, and hopefully see the positive effects that you expect, it will become easier to be consistent with the target behaviour.

Critically, if for some reason you don't manage to do the new activity on any given day it doesn't matter. There is no need to recriminate with yourself. Similarly, nothing is broken – the transgression is simply a part of the process of instilling your new habit. You should then use the minor hiccup as motivation to ensure that you perform the new activity at the next suitable opportunity. In this way "failure" can be the source of further motivation, rather than being a reason to entirely abandon a way of living that you have decided you want to follow.

Finally, it is worth noting that sometimes taking a break is the best way to ensure long term consistency of training and thus paradoxically is the right thing to do with regards to the cardinal rule of training. Sometimes you just need to take a day off, and getting out and training would be counterproductive due to increased risk of injury or overtraining or simply reduced motivation.

15.8. Goals

Much has been written on goal setting, and so I just want to give a very quick sketch of what I feel are the important points here. One should realise that the training process is inherently about the identification of training goals and then following a plan to achieve them. There are probably three principles relating to goal setting that are especially important in the training context:

- It is great to have ambitious long term goals however such goals are not very effective in maintaining your day to day motivation and consistency. Make sure that you break down your long term goals into a series of realistic and achievable short and medium term goals;

- It is more effective to set process orientated goals as opposed to outcome orientated goals. In training it is very easy to fall into the trap of setting performance goals (e.g. I want to run this time or lift this weight). It is more productive to identify the behaviours that you will need to exhibit to reach such a performance level, and to base your goals around displaying these behaviours;
- Try to have a "growth" mindset. We have already talked about the importance of expectation in this chapter. A growth mindset is one where you believe that your abilities are very malleable and that they can be enhanced considerably through training, as opposed to a fixed mindset where you believe that your abilities are largely predetermined and not that amenable to change.

15.9. Curiosity cost the cat his gains

One of the most admirable traits of humans is our inquisitiveness. We like to explore, to learn new things and to try out new ideas. Unfortunately this is a real threat to the training process. This can be manifested in a number of ways, as described below.

The fact that you are reading (and have got this far through) this book is evidence that training is interesting to you. One problem with training is that there is a gigantic number of different ways of achieving a particular goal. There is a natural tendency for people who are interested in training to keep trying out these different training methods. This can then lead a person to violate the cardinal rule of training – that is, that a person doesn't train consistently because they keep switching training programmes, goals or methods. Another way of characterising this problem is that training the same way for many months or years can get boring for people, either physically or intellectually, or both. This can then prompt a desire to train different things.

> "It worked so well, I didn't do it again."
>
> Dan John

A similar problem is caused by the common human need to invent. Again, this can lead a person to seek new ways of training when the methods that they are using are still working. A good example of this is the popularity of dynamic systems theory (DST) that has gained some traction recently in strength and conditioning circles (and which I referred to in Chapter 9.7). Many practitioners now describe training in the language of DST without really understanding the concepts they are referring to – but the "posh" language and the new concepts satisfy their intellectual needs. Less scrupulous practitioners also recognise the powerful marketing value of cultivating themselves as a "guru" by using impenetrable pseudoscientific language. At the level of training, a focus on a DST based theory of training has impelled some practitioners to create and use new exercises that are either unproven or that to some degree violate existing guidelines for picking exercises – while at the same time moving away from tried and tested methods of training.

"Adeo nihil motum ex antique probabile est: It is probable that nothing has changed since the time of the ancients."

Titus Livius

The preceding discussion is not meant to suggest that innovation should be avoided. Rather we should always be seeking improvements to things that we are doing. However, we need to recognise the value of tried and tested methods that have worked for us, or that are well supported by the experience of previous athletes and coaches, and by established training theory. The majority of our programme should be consistent (as suggested by the cardinal rule of training), and our innovation and experimentation should represent only a small proportion of our training.

15.10. Egotism and invention

In the previous section we talked about the threats to a successful training programme that arise due to the human need to explore. These problems can be exacerbated by an individual's ego, especially if they have a need to feel like an expert.

A good example of this is the concept of "the aggregation of marginal gains" which has been widely credited for the success of British sporting teams in the 2012 and 2016 Olympics. This concept is based on the conceit that these elite programmes are so good that the only way to find improvements is to constantly hunt the "1%s", and if enough of these are found that they can provide a winning edge. A similar argument based upon Pareto's Principle would be that we are doing the most important 20% so well that we will scour the remaining 80% for places where we can make small improvements. Almost without exception (in sport at least) adherents of the "marginal gains philosophy" are deceiving themselves when they think they are doing the 20% perfectly. In my experience in elite sport, working with the same organisations that tout the importance of marginal gains, the most important parts of the programme are very far from perfect. The focus on seeking these marginal gains thus becomes highly counterproductive – big flaws in the programme are left unchallenged while coaches hunt for places where they can make tiny improvements.

16 HOW TO COMPETE

16.1. The relationship between training and competition

It may seem obvious, but it is worth explicitly stating that the aim of training is generally to improve an athlete's performance capability within the competitive environment. Medals are not awarded for training performances. This is an important fact that should be highly influential in training choices but people are often distracted from their focus on it. In particular, a common mistake is to set too much stock in the training performance itself.

Of course, if your training is not based on a competitive goal it is entirely fine to realise your best performances in training.

16.2. Trust your preparation

> "Keep sharpening your knife and it will blunt."
>
> Lao Tzu, Te Tao Ching

It is common for athletes to gain confidence from their training – knowing that you have performed a solid block of training and have increased your performance capability should make you optimistic about the outcome of a competition. However, this reliance on practice and training as a source of confidence can be taken too far. This is evident in athletes who have a need to indulge in extensive training sessions in the immediate run up to a competition. This can clearly be counter-productive, as there is a serious risk that the athlete will either not be in peak condition or be fatigued for the competition itself.

Steve Magness gives an interesting example of an athlete who has a more positive relationship with his preparation that is taken from the world of baseball.

"When Lance McCullers took the mound for the Houston Astros in game 7 of the World Series, he hadn't thrown a single curveball since he stepped off the mound 5 days earlier after game 3 of the series. To McCullers, the curveball isn't just another pitch, it's his signature one. He throws it more than any other pitcher in baseball; an astonishing 47 percent of all the pitches McCullers throws are the curve. Yet, according to broadcaster and Hall of Fame pitcher John Smoltz, McCullers didn't practice throwing the curve during his practice sessions between games, or even his warm-ups. McCullers knows how to throw the curve. He has confidence in it."

Steve Magness, 08/11/17, www.peakperformancebook.net

A particularly egregious example of not trusting your preparation is represented in the athlete who needs to "test" their performance capability prior to the event, for instance by performing a maximum squat attempt in the 2 weeks preceding a powerlifting competition. As we have seen, the attainment of a peak is a delicate process, with a potentially large drop off after it has been reached. There is the real danger that athletes who test their performance capability in this way actually go over the peak in training, compromising their performance. This leads to the training maxim that one should save something for the platform (or track, or pitch, or lake...). One should aim to peak during competition often without having gone to maximal effort beforehand.

16.3. Train to compete

A common training mistake is to train to improve performance capability under ideal conditions. For instance, a middle distance runner might train to be able to run the fastest possible evenly-paced mile (the physiologically optimal strategy) or a powerlifter might train to be able to be able to pull the biggest possible deadlift they can in the gym. The problem with this approach is that competition doesn't normally take place in ideal conditions.

One aspect of competition that is very different to training is the fact that you will have competitors and they will try to manipulate the competitive environment to gain advantage. For instance, a competitive mile is unlikely to be run at an even pace. Those athletes who believe that they have a greater top speed will try to slow the early part of the race to preserve their sprint finish. Conversely, the fittest athletes will try to make the race more physiologically challenging, for instance by steadily increasing the pace or by varying the pace – speeding up and slowing down repeatedly. To this end it behoves an athlete to develop the physiological capacities that are required to race in these different ways. Of course, a thorough needs analysis should have identified these requirements.

However it is not enough to just be physiologically prepared for any eventuality in racing, the athlete also has to be psychologically prepared to compete. They need to practise being in different racing situations, and to learn how to win in a variety of different ways and from different positions. These skills can be practised in less important competitions or within training.

Another major difference in competition is that the conditions are not under the athlete's control. For example, for the aforementioned mile runner, there are likely to be constraints on the way in which the athlete is able to warm up. In particular, prior to their race they will be held in a call room where they will have limited opportunity to perform any type of physical exercise. Similarly, once they are called to the track they will have very little time available to them to re-warm up. Thus, no matter how well the athlete is able to warm up prior to entering the call room (and there will likely be constraints on this too), by the time they reach the track their preparation will have been impaired.

For the example of the powerlifter that was mentioned earlier, training to pull a big deadlift in the gym when fresh similarly doesn't reflect the actual demands of competition. In powerlifting, the deadlift is the third lift that is completed, after the squat and bench. By the time the athlete comes to deadlift they will already have performed maximal efforts in 2 whole body exercises. Preparation for an excellent deadlift performance in competition thus needs to recognise this, and the athlete needs to train such that they are still able to perform maximally under considerable fatigue.

A further difference between training and competition is that in competition we will often be performing under considerable stress. Again, the thoughtful athlete will train such that they can still perform skills under pressure. It is a self-limiting fallacy to think that you can't prepare for the special demands of competition. An example of the propagation of this fallacy can be found when listening to MMA pundits who often opine that you can't prepare for the "adrenaline dump" that you can experience when first stepping into the Octagon to compete in the UFC. The same commentators also often suggest that punching power is an innate capacity that can't be trained!

16.4. Nerves

"One is a great deal less anxious if one feels perfectly free to be anxious."

Alan W. Watts

Many people are badly hampered by nerves during competitive (and other) performances. However, being nervous is a perfectly normal and natural part of competition. Being nervous is not a negative state, and there is no reason at all why suffering from nerves should be detrimental to your performance. Why then are some people more able to handle nervousness than others?

I am absolutely convinced that the answer to this question is encapsulated in Alan Watts' quote above. In particular, the problem is not being nervous, but rather it is the reaction of the athlete to feeling nervous. As Watts says, if you accept the fact that you will be nervous during competition then nervousness is not normally a problem – and paradoxically your nervousness will probably diminish as you compete.

Problems can arise if an athlete reacts to feeling nervous. There are two common negative reactions. The first is that the athlete dislikes the feeling of being nervous and tries to stop it. This is a futile battle and is somewhat akin to the psychological challenge of trying not to think about something (the classic example is a white bear). The harder you try not to think of a white bear, the more likely you are to think of it. The same applies with nervousness. The more you try to not be nervous, and the more you evaluate the nervousness as a bad thing, the worse you suffer.

The second negative reaction is when an athlete links nerves with poor performance. If they then experience nervousness they start to worry that it will negatively affect their performance. This then increases the anxiety, and brings the athlete's focus to the nervousness, exacerbating the problem.

The "secret" to dealing with performance anxiety is simply to recognise that nerves are just a feeling. The experience may be unpleasant, but it will not be harmful. If you can learn to accept that you will be anxious, but not attribute any negative consequences to it, and not try to avoid it, then it ceases to be a problem.

Often when an athlete is nervous a coach will tell them to relax. This is terrible advice – you can't force relaxation if feeling nervous – this is fighting nervousness in the way described above.

17 HOW TO COACH

17.1. Introduction

The majority of this book has been addressed to either athlete or coach. The purpose of this chapter is to draw out some specific examples of how the principles outlined in the preceding chapters can be applied to the coaching process, alongside some other advice for coaches.

In this chapter I will mainly address the following 4 overlapping functions of the coach. Of course, this is not to suggest that this is an exclusive list.

- Providing support to the athlete (emotional, cognitive, material, etc);
- Teaching movement skills;
- Prescribing and overseeing training sessions that are designed to improve performance capabilities;
- Giving competitive advice (including tactical advice) both during and outside of competition.

17.2. Care! (support)

> "People don't care how much you know until they know how much you care."
>
> Theodore Roosevelt

The above quote, which is generally attributed to Theodore Roosevelt, is referred to so frequently that it is at risk of becoming a platitude. However, there are few lessons that are of such profound importance for a coach. I always worry about coaches who describe one of their strengths as being their ability to relate to and motivate their athletes. For me, this ability should be a given for any aspiring coach, and if it is not something that comes naturally then it should be absolutely the first developmental priority.

It is quite common for people who are passionate about sport to be both athletes and coaches. This is an entirely natural consequence of people immersing themselves in their interests and/or wanting to make a living from them. However, I do think it is worth observing that for most people it is impossible to give their all to both coaching and competing. In particular, situations will frequently arise when there is a conflict between the needs of the coach (in relation to their own sporting endeavours) and the athletes that they coach. For instance, both training and coaching are highly demanding of our finite energy reserves and a coach-athlete will either need to conserve energy during coaching in order to train effectively, or will need to accept a subpar training session.

As a coach I think it is important to be aware of this fact, and to adjust your behaviour accordingly. If your goal is first and foremost to be the most effective coach that you can be then you need to accept the fact that your training and competition performance might sometimes need to take a back seat to that of your athletes. If you are unwilling to sacrifice your own performances on the altar of your athletes' performances that is of course entirely fine. However, you need to recognise the limitations that this will place on your ability to coach, and be honest with both yourself and your athletes about it.

17.3. Understand the importance of life outside sport (support)

If we are lucky, then we eventually come to the realisation that there are more important things within life than our sporting performance. This doesn't mean that training to improve performance capability isn't a valid goal. However, it does mean that the training process, the process of competing, or the rewards from competition should enrich our lives. A coach who truly cares about the athlete, and not the prestige associated with high performance, will understand this, and will coach in a way that will help fulfil the athlete.

This is not to argue that the training process shouldn't be hard, or that sacrifices shouldn't be made. It is just that coach and athlete should be sure that the potential rewards will be appropriate compensation for these sacrifices. For instance, coaches should recognise that for some individuals a college scholarship or a career as a professional athlete might be their only realistic chance of escaping the poverty trap. In these situations very great sacrifices might be justified. At the same time however, the coach should ensure that the athlete's self esteem is not too entangled with their sporting ability, and that they still develop within all important domains.

The above situation is probably the exception to the rule however. For most athletes the intrinsic rewards of training or competing should be compensation for training hard or making sacrifices. In many cases this will mean that the process of training itself should have a positive influence on an athlete's life generally.

17.4. Give good cues (teaching skills)

A popular area within sports science research is that of the effectiveness of coaching cues. In particular, sports scientists have been interested in the effect of the "focus of attention" on sporting performance. A distinction has been made between cues that are focussed on the external environment (e.g. if coaching a vertical jump, to cue the athlete to jump and touch a point on the wall that is as high as possible) and cues that are focussed internally (e.g. extend your knees and hips as fast as possible).

There is quite a compelling body of literature that suggests that externally focussed cues are more effective in enhancing performance, and hypotheses have been advanced to explain this phenomenon[39]. Most of this research shows a fundamental lack of understanding of the coaching process – that is that (hopefully) athletes will tend to try and do what you tell them to do, and so you need to make sure that the cue that you give is appropriate. For instance, in the above example I contrasted 2 different cues that could be given to an athlete to help them perform a vertical jump. The research on focus of attention has found that the instruction for an athlete to reach as high as possible produces a higher vertical jump than the instruction to extend the knees and hips fast, and has explained this fact by reference to the fact that the former cue is external. There is a much simpler explanation – only the first cue specifies that the athlete should jump as high as they can. In fact, a former student of mine found that athletes who were given the latter cue, extended their knees and hips faster than when they were given the former cue[3]. That is, they did exactly what they were cued to do and the reason that they jumped less high is just that they were being cued to use a less effective movement strategy.

Another good example of poor coaching can be seen when coaches teach athletes to squat. A very common cue that is given to athletes to help them squat is to push their hips backwards to initiate the movement. This is a good cue for athletes who naturally see squatting simply as a deep knee bend as it encourages them to use their hips. However, it is important to recognise that an athlete can't keep pushing their hips backwards as they squat deeper or they will fall over (Figure 17.4). However, it is really common to see coaches encourage athletes to "squat deeper, push your hips back, now get deeper...". For compliant athletes – that is athletes who faithfully try to follow the cues they are being given – this leads to a situation which is highly frustrating. No matter how hard they try the athlete will not be able to get deeper using the strategy that is being cued – to do so would mean they fall over.

Figure 17.4. Continuing to push the hips back during squatting will unbalance the athlete backwards.

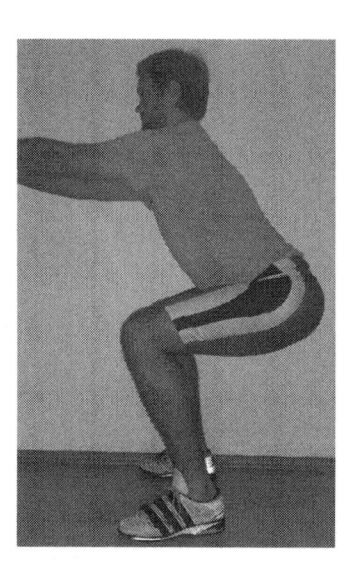

As coaches therefore we need to be very careful about the cues that we give to our athletes. We need to be cognizant of the fact that we can hamper our athlete's learning of a skill if we give them unhelpful cues. This in turn is one reason why using some of the strategies described in Chapter 9 that encourage athletes to solve problems for themselves can be beneficial.

Giving effective cues can often require a profound understanding of the movement in question. It is not enough to simply have a mental picture of how the movement should look – this just allows you to identify that something doesn't look right, but gives no basis for effective error correction. Instead, a coach needs to understand the imperatives that determine the way that different movements are performed, such that they know the reason why a movement might be performed in a non-optimal way. Once the "why" of the movement error is known, the coach also needs to understand what part of the skill needs to be changed to improve the movement – the error that is spotted may be a result of something that happens before or after the error itself is seen. Finally the coach needs to experiment with different ways of cueing an athlete to find out which ones are most effective for helping the athlete to change the movement in the desired way. It is also useful if the coach has multiple options for this – has a "go-to" cue that works in most cases, but also has other alternatives if a given cue doesn't work for an individual.

17.5. Don't blame the athlete or exercise (teaching skills)

A personal bugbear of mine is the tendency of S&C coaches to blame an athlete's inability to perform a given movement to the standard that they desire on "anatomical limitations". Thus, the reason that their athlete cannot squat deep with good form is "because they have limited ankle or hip range of motion" etc. I believe that we are far too quick to blame our athletes' problems on anything apart from ourselves. If our athlete struggles to squat, absolutely our first port of call should be to ask ourselves if they are struggling because we are not coaching them well enough. One aspect of this is whether we are providing good cues as discussed in the previous section.

More generally, if an athlete is unable to learn a skill, or to improve a given capacity, we should first examine our own practice to look for the source of the problem. Of course, it is entirely possible that an athlete is limited by their anatomy, is dyspraxic (has difficulty learning physical skills), is a hard gainer (is genetically limited in their ability to gain muscle) etc. However, too often these types of explanations are used by coaches as easy get outs that mean they don't need to confront the truth that maybe their practice is the root of the problem.

A similar situation sometimes arises when coaches are vigorous critics of a given training modality. For instance, in Chapter 10.12 I described how some coaches are strongly opposed to the use of Olympic weightlifting exercises in training. One common criticism of these exercises is that they are highly technical and take a long time to learn. For me, this is an example of the coach blaming the exercise, rather than taking a hard look at their own abilities. There is nothing intrinsically inherent to Olympic weightlifting that requires them to take a long time to learn. Rather, skilled coaches can generally very quickly teach athletes to use weightlifting derivatives as effective training tools. A fairer statement from a coach who finds Olympic weightlifting too technical would be that it takes him too long to teach his athletes how to Olympic weightlift. The problem is not with the exercise, but the skill of the coach. Again, a coach should make sure that they properly understand a training activity before they discount its value.

17.6. Keeping it interesting (prescribing sessions)

There is a real danger that a focus on adhering to the cardinal rule of training can be self defeating. That is, the cardinal rule tells us that training should be consistent, and one interpretation of this is that we need to do similar things for a long time. For many people this ultimately can become boring – and boredom is a threat to consistent training. Thus the role of the coach will often be to come up with training activities and plans that are essentially the same, but that feel new and different to the athlete. A good example is the use of running drills. Running drills are used in the training of track and field athletes to improve their running capabilities, essentially by practising (and emphasising) one or other aspect of running technique and doing it a lot. To this end, track and field coaches have created a gigantic number of running drills, which in their essence simply represent many variations on a couple of very limited themes.

Similarly, coaching is often a process of nagging. Elite athletes can spend a large amount of time perfecting skills, where to the untrained eye there is very little change in the appearance of the movement. Consequently, the coach can spend many sessions trying to help the athlete do a particular thing within a given skill. Essentially, the coaching process is then about reiterating the same message in new ways, to maintain interest and hopefully encourage the "light bulb" moment. Even when an athlete has learned a skill, the same messages often need to be routinely reinforced – nagging again.

17.7. Most of the time it is about holding athletes back (prescribing sessions)

One of the key theses of this book has been the idea that a very large proportion of our training should be performed "within ourselves". In particular, in Chapter 6.4 I contended that the number one training error that people make is to train moderately hard all of the time, without any great variation in the intensity they train at. I have been at pains in this book to show that very many training sessions should be easy for the athlete to perform. This is a hard message for people to accept – we are constantly bombarded by the notion that we can achieve anything with hard work (I addressed how this is a myth when applied to training in Chapter 15.3).

It is particularly difficult for highly motivated athletes to accept and trust the idea that they are often training too hard. The role of the coach then is most often to "hold an athlete back". This is almost directly opposite to the common stereotype of the coach as a merciless slave driver constantly exhorting the athlete to greater and greater efforts. I would argue that in a great many cases, one of the greatest benefits that a coach can provide to an athlete is in giving them the confidence to train within themselves. Such a course of action often requires a great deal of support, as the behaviour is so contrary to the messages about the importance of hard work that the athlete will have heard from a young age.

During a given cycle the challenges are as follows. Firstly, the coach will need to help the athlete to pick a volume and intensity of training at the start of the cycle that is light enough (erring on the side of being too light). Secondly, as the athlete gets towards the middle of the training cycle they will start to fly – everything will be easy. At this point the coach needs to work hard to rein in the athlete – and to guard against progressing too quickly. Finally, towards the end of cycle it may be necessary to give the athlete some support to train at higher volumes or intensities. Throughout training, coach and athlete need to be aware of the temptation to "see what they can do" – these tests should largely be saved for the competitive environment.

17.8. Technical/tactical advice

If you are the sport coach of an athlete then of course you will regularly be involved in providing technical/tactical advice to your athletes (Figure 17.8). However, if you are a strength and conditioning or fitness coach, you can still play a role in helping athletes in this area. In particular, the general training environment can be a powerful arena for learning and practising both general and specific competitive skills. In fact, sometimes it can be a more beneficial area for experimenting with new strategies as the athlete will not carry the baggage that might be associated with risking under performance in their sport itself.

Figure 17.8. Coaching conversations.

In Dan John's writing and teaching he emphasises a good example of the type of skills that can be practised in the training environment - that is the ability to regulate arousal. As we saw in Chapter 14.2 the optimal level of arousal will differ between different skills. An athlete who is skilful at competing will be able to easily and voluntarily find the optimal level of arousal. Moreover, the skilful athlete will be able to do this without an over-reliance on external input (e.g. the use of aggressive music in order to "psyche up"). Playing with different levels of arousal is something that is easy to do in the training environment, and the skills developed in training seem likely to be transferable to competition.

17.9. Look after yourself

You do your athletes a disservice if you don't ensure that you have time for yourself. If you work too hard then the quality of the work you do will be impaired. More importantly, you deserve a life yourself – the notion that we should sacrifice ourselves for our jobs (especially if it is your passion) is just another manifestation of the misguided thinking that leads to the "give 100% all the time" mentality.

CONCLUSION

An important concept in medicine, health and fitness is that what we do should be "evidence based". Ultimately, what this means is that we should have a reason for what we do that amounts to more than simply tradition or unsupported opinion. Broadly, the evidence for practice is instead drawn from the scientific literature and clinical practice, and should reflect the athlete's values.

Most people struggle with understanding how to incorporate scientific literature into their practice. The problem arises because they look for specific research studies that have investigated the specific tool or application that they are interested in. This is generally not a viable strategy in training – the response to training is highly multi-factorial and there is such a gigantic variety of possible approaches. Instead, the role of science is to provide the broad theoretical basis for training practice.

Training theory however is also limited – it can be used (entirely correctly) to justify any number of approaches. The art of coaching is then in finding the most effective approaches that are suggested by the theory. Experience is indispensable in this exercise in providing context to the theory, and as a source of evidence of what works (for you) in the real world. However, the most important step in developing the art of coaching is thinking about it.

A key argument in this book is that training programmes should consist of mainly light and heavy sessions – this is not a new idea. In the scientific literature and some training publications this method is sometimes called polarised training. However, I have deliberately not referred to polarised training or this evidence within this book. There is some scientific evidence that supports its efficacy in endurance training[29,31]. A recent article stated that their data "provide supportive rationale for the polarised model of training, showing the training phases with increased time spent at high-intensity suppress parasympathetic activity, whilst low-intensity training preserves and increases it"[29]. I don't know what this means. Quite possibly this is a mechanism which contributes to the effectiveness of the approach. However, it is not necessary to appeal to this evidence in order to justify the approach that I describe here. Similarly, the training theory from which I derive my justification is much more useful in actually working out what an athlete should be doing. I don't know where I would start if I started explicitly trying to write training programmes where I tried to increase or decrease an athlete's parasympathetic activity.

At the start of this book I talked about the sophistication inherent within simplicity. Great coaches help their athletes by doing things that are easy to understand – and the elegance in what they do is easy to miss. I was once lucky enough to watch Dan John coaching a national level heptathlete in the shot put. He increased the distance of her throw by 50cm in about 5 seconds. She always started her throw at the back of the throwing circle. The same circle is used by all athletes, and so needs to accommodate a gigantic male shot putter too. Consequently there is more space than a 60kg female heptathlete using a glide technique needs and the heptathlete was releasing the shot 50cm short of the front of the circle. So Dan moved her start point forwards!

The most important thing to realise in the above story is that this heptathlete was a proficient thrower already. She lives and breathes athletics and has been coached by some of UK's most high status coaches. However, none of these coaches had ever made this simple adjustment. Why not? Because they are attracted to the advanced, complicated or technical not the simple but effective.

In this book I have outlined and justified what I understand to be the principles that underpin a successful training programme. The key messages of this book can be boiled down to 3 principles:

1. The cardinal rule of training and its corollary: that is, be consistent and don't do things that will prejudice your consistency;
2. The training week should mainly consist of relatively light "practice" sessions but with 2 or 3 more intense "GAS focused" training sessions;
3. Medium to long term planning should be focused on "base building" and "building up".

I have argued that the number one error that people make in training is to train moderately hard all of the time, as opposed to having lots of light practice sessions interspersed with more intense hot sessions. This is not to say that training hard all the time can't be effective. However, it takes deep reserves of will power to stick to such a programme – particularly when trying to train hard when you are already tired. In contrast, if following the approach described here, after our practice sessions we should feel better physically and mentally, and we should have the energy to really attack (and potentially work hard) in our hot sessions. Ultimately, it seems easier to adhere to the cardinal rule of training if you enjoy and look forward to the majority of your training sessions, and this is thus more likely to encourage progress. Or at least, that is what I think.

REFERENCES

1. Aagaard, P., Simonsen, E. B., Andersen, J. L., Magnusson, P. & Dyhre-Poulsen, P. Increased rate of force development and neural drive of human skeletal muscle following resistance training. *J Appl Physiol* 93, 1318–1326 (2002).

2. Bannister, E. W. Modeling elite athletic performance. In *Physiological Testing of Elite Athletes (eds. MacDougall, J. D., Wenger, H. A. & Green, H. J.).* (Human Kinetics, 1991).

3. Barnard, L. Effect of different internal and external cues on countermovement jump kinematics and kinetics: Specific cue more influential than attentional focus. *MSc Dissertation* (2018).

4. Barnes, K. R. Comparisons of perceived training doses in champion collegiate-level male and female cross-country runners and coaches over the course of a competitive season. *Sports Med - Open* 3, 38 (2017).

5. Bernstein, N. A. *The Co-ordination and Regulation of Movements.* (Pergamon Press, 1967).

6. Blagrove, R. C., Howatson, G. & Hayes, P. R. Effects of strength training on the physiological determinants of middle- and long-distance running performance: A systematic review. *Sports Med* 48, 1117–1149 (2018).

7. Blickhan, R. The spring-mass model for running and hopping. *J Biomech* 22, 1217–1227 (1989).

8. Bobbert, M. F. & van Soest, A. J. Why do people jump the way they do? *Exerc Sport Sci Rev* 29, 95–102 (2001).

9. Borg, G. A. Psychophysical bases of perceived exertion. *Med Sci Sports Exerc* 14, 377–381 (1982).

10. Bowers, R. W. & Fox, E. L. *Sports Physiology*. (William C Brown Pub, 1992).

11. Colagiuri, B., Schenk, L. A., Kessler, M. D., Dorsey, S. G. & Colloca, L. The placebo effect: From concepts to genes. *Neuroscience* 307, 171–190 (2015).

12. Conley, D. L. & Krahenbuhl, G. S. Running economy and distance running performance of highly trained athletes. *Med Sci Sports Exerc* 12, 357–360 (1980).

13. De Lorme, T. L. & Watkins, A. L. *Progressive Resistance Exercise: Technique and Medical Application*. (Appleton-Century-Crofts, 1951).

14. Drechsler, A. J. *The Weightlifting Encyclopedia: A Guide to World Class Performance*. (A is A communications, 1998).

15. Fitts, P. M. & Posner, M. I. *Human Performance*. (Brooks/Cole, 1967).

16. Gladwell, M. *Outliers: The Story of Success*. (Back Bay Books, 2011).

17. Goodwin, J. E. & Cleather, D. J. The biomechanical principles underpinning strength and conditioning. In *Strength and Conditioning for Sports Performance (eds. Jeffreys, I. & Moody, J.)*. (Routledge, 2016).

18. Gould, D. & Udry, E. Psychological skills for enhancing performance: arousal regulation strategies. *Med Sci Sports Exerc* 26, 478–485 (1994).

19. Grobler, J. Preparation - Rio 2016 - Training, Technique & Selection - GBR Open Men. *Presentation*.

20. Hackett, D., Davies, T., Soomro, N. & Halaki, M. Olympic weightlifting training improves vertical jump height in sportspeople: A systematic review with meta-analysis. *Br J Sports Med* 50, 865–872 (2016).

21. Hadim, M. StrongLifts 5×5 workout program for beginners. *StrongLifts*. Downloaded from https://stronglifts.com/5x5/ in July 2018.

22. Sheppard, J. M. & Triplett, N. T. Program design for resistance training. In *Essentials of Strength Training and Conditioning 4th Edition (eds. Haff, G. & Triplett, N. T.)*. (Human Kinetics Australia P/L, 2015).

23. Jackson, M. Evaluating the role of Hans Selye in the modern history of stress. In *Stress, Shock, and Adaptation in the Twentieth Century (eds. Cantor, D. & Ramsden, E.)* (University of Rochester Press, 2014).

24. Lucia, A. *et al.* Physiological characteristics of the best Eritrean runners—exceptional running economy. *Appl Physiol Nutr Metab* 31, 530–540 (2006).

25. Magill, R. A. & Hall, K. G. A review of the contextual interference effect in motor skill acquisition. *Human Mov Sci* 9, 241–289 (1990).

26. Matveyev, L. P. *Fundamentals of Sports Training (A. P. Zdornykh, Trans.)*. (Moscow, Russia: Fizkultura i Spovt, 1977).

27. Medvedyev, A. S. *A System of Multi-Year Training in Weightlifting (A. Charniga, Trans.)*. (Moscow, Russia: Fizkultura i Spovt, 1986).

28. Nilsen, T. S. FISA Training Program for Clubs and Individuals. (2009).

29. Plews, D. J., Laursen, P. B., Kilding, A. E. & Buchheit, M. Heart-rate variability and training-intensity distribution in elite rowers. *Int J Sports Phys Perf* 9, 1026–1032 (2014).

30. Reilly, T. & Edwards, B. Altered sleep–wake cycles and physical performance in athletes. *Phys Behav* 90, 274–284 (2007).

31. Rosenblat, M. A., Perrotta, A. S. & Vicenzino, B. Polarized vs. threshold training intensity distribution on endurance sport performance: A systematic review and meta-analysis of randomized controlled trials. *J Strength Cond Res* in press (2018).

32. Santos-Concejero, J. *et al.* Gait-cycle characteristics and running economy in elite Eritrean and European runners. *Int J Sports Physiol Perform* 10, 381–387 (2015).

33. Selye, H. A syndrome produced by diverse nocuous agents. *Nature* 138, 32 (1936).

34. Siff, M. C. *Supertraining (6th Edition)*. (Supertraining Institute, 2003).

35. Tsatsouline, P. Another Russian super cycle. *www.dragondoor.com* (2002).

36. Wendler, J. *5/3/1 for Powerlifting: Simple and Effective Training for Maximal Strength*. (Jim Wendler LLC, Ohio, 2011).

37. Weyand, P. G., Sternlight, D. B., Bellizzi, M. J. & Wright, S. Faster top running speeds are achieved with greater ground forces not more rapid leg movements. *J Appl Physiol* 89, 1991–1999 (2000).

38. Wood, P. P., Goodwin, J. E. & Cleather, D. J. Lighter and heavier initial loads yield similar gains in strength when employing a progressive wave loading scheme. *Biol of Sport* 33, 257–261 (2016).

39. Wulf, G. & Lewthwaite, R. Optimizing performance through intrinsic motivation and attention for learning: The OPTIMAL theory of motor learning. *Psychon Bull Rev* 23, 1382–1414 (2016).

40. Zeinalov, A. A. Methods of developing leg strength (translated by A. Charniga). *Tiazhelaya Atletika* 29–31 (1976).

ABOUT THE AUTHOR

Dan is a Reader in Strength and Conditioning and Programme Director of the MSc in Strength and Conditioning at St Mary's University, Twickenham, UK. Before joining St Mary's he was employed as a strength and conditioning coach at the English Institute of Sport. He began his coaching career as a volunteer assistant strength and conditioning coach at California State University Long Beach. Dan has coached national and international medallists across a wide range of sports, and in particular has worked with World and Olympic champions in track and field athletics, rowing, canoeing and rugby. Dan's PhD is in biomedical engineering (from Imperial College London) and his research interests include musculoskeletal modelling, functional anatomy and strength training. He has published around 40 articles in peer reviewed scientific and professional practice journals. He is a founder member of the UK Strength and Conditioning Association and currently serves the organisation as Director of Finance and Administration (a post he also held between 2005 and 2009).